The Peace Corps

KNOW YOUR GOVERNMENT

The Peace Corps

Madeline Weitsman

CHELSEA HOUSE PUBLISHERS

On the cover: A Peace Corps volunteer teaches nutrition education in Micronesia.
Frontis: A Peace Corps volunteer walks with village women to get water from a well
in Gambia.

Chelsea House Publishers
Editor-in-Chief: Nancy Toff
Executive Editor: Remmel T. Nunn
Managing Editor: Karyn Gullen Browne
Copy Chief: Juliann Barbato
Picture Editor: Adrian G. Allen
Art Director: Maria Epes
Manufacturing Manager: Gerald Levine

Know Your Government
Senior Editor: Kathy Kuhtz

Staff for THE PEACE CORPS
Assistant Editor: Gillian Bucky
Copy Editor: Lisa S. Fenev
Deputy Copy Chief: Nicole Bowen
Editorial Assistant: Elizabeth Nix
Picture Coordinator: Michèle Brisson
Picture Researcher: Dixon and Turner Research Associates, Inc.
Assistant Art Director: Loraine Machlin
Senior Designer: Noreen M. Lamb
Production Coordinator: Joseph Romano

3 5 7 9 8 6 4 2

Library of Congress Cataloging-in-Publication Data
Weitsman, Madeline.
  The Peace Corps / Madeline Weitsman.
    p. cm.—(Know your government)
  Bibliography: p.
  Includes index.
  1. Peace Corps (U.S.) I. Title. II. Series: Know your government (New York, N.Y.)
  HC60.5.W424 1989
  361.2′6′06073—dc19
    ISBN 0-87754-832-3   88-38228
      0-7910-0903-3(pbk.)   CIP

CONTENTS

Introduction   7

1 An Eloquent Challenge   15

2 Armies of Peace   21

3 A Triumphal Beginning   39

4 Growing Pains   59

5 Today's Peace Corps   79

6 The Men and Women of the Peace Corps   97

7 The Peace Corps in the Future   113

Organizational Chart Peace Corps   117

Glossary   118

Selected References   119

Index   121

KNOW YOUR GOVERNMENT

The American Red Cross

The Bureau of Indian Affairs

The Central Intelligence Agency

The Commission on Civil Rights

The Department of Agriculture

The Department of the Air Force

The Department of the Army

The Department of Commerce

The Department of Defense

The Department of Education

The Department of Energy

The Department of Health and
Human Services

The Department of Housing and
Urban Development

The Department of the Interior

The Department of Justice

The Department of Labor

The Department of the Navy

The Department of State

The Department of Transportation

The Department of the Treasury

The Drug Enforcement Administration

The Environmental Protection Agency

The Equal Employment
Opportunity Commission

The Federal Aviation Administration

The Federal Bureau of Investigation

The Federal Communications Commission

The Federal Government: How it Works

The Federal Reserve System

The Federal Trade Commission

The Food and Drug Administration

The Forest Service

The House of Representatives

The Immigration and Naturalization Service

The Internal Revenue Service

The Library of Congress

The National Aeronautics and Space
Administration

The National Archives and Records
Administration

The National Foundation on the Arts
and the Humanities

The National Park Service

The National Science Foundation

The Nuclear Regulatory Commission

The Peace Corps

The Presidency

The Public Health Service

The Securities and Exchange Commission

The Senate

The Small Business Administration

The Smithsonian

The Supreme Court

The Tennessee Valley Authority

The U.S. Arms Control and
Disarmament Agency

The U.S. Coast Guard

The U.S. Constitution

The U.S. Fish and Wildlife Service

The U.S. Information Agency

The U.S. Marine Corps

The U.S. Mint

The U.S. Postal Service

The U.S. Secret Service

The Veterans Administration

CHELSEA HOUSE PUBLISHERS

Government: Crises of Confidence

Arthur M. Schlesinger, jr.

From the start, Americans have regarded their government with a mixture of reliance and mistrust. The men who founded the republic did not doubt the indispensability of government. "If men were angels," observed the 51st Federalist Paper, "no government would be necessary." But men are not angels. Because human beings are subject to wicked as well as to noble impulses, government was deemed essential to assure freedom and order.

At the same time, the American revolutionaries knew that government could also become a source of injury and oppression. The men who gathered in Philadelphia in 1787 to write the Constitution therefore had two purposes in mind. They wanted to establish a strong central authority and to limit that central authority's capacity to abuse its power.

To prevent the abuse of power, the Founding Fathers wrote two basic principles into the new Constitution. The principle of federalism divided power between the state governments and the central authority. The principle of the separation of powers subdivided the central authority itself into three branches—the executive, the legislative, and the judiciary—so that "each may be a check on the other." The *Know Your Government* series focuses on the major executive departments and agencies in these branches of the federal government.

The Constitution did not plan the executive branch in any detail. After vesting the executive power in the president, it assumed the existence of "executive departments" without specifying what these departments should be. Congress began defining their functions in 1789 by creating the Departments of State, Treasury, and War. The secretaries in charge of these departments made up President Washington's first cabinet. Congress also provided for a legal officer, and President Washington soon invited the attorney general, as he was called, to attend cabinet meetings. As need required, Congress created more executive departments.

Setting up the cabinet was only the first step in organizing the American state. With almost no guidance from the Constitution, President Washington, seconded by Alexander Hamilton, his brilliant secretary of the treasury, equipped the infant republic with a working administrative structure. The Federalists believed in both executive energy and executive accountability and set high standards for public appointments. The Jeffersonian opposition had less faith in strong government and preferred local government to the central authority. But when Jefferson himself became president in 1801, although he set out to change the direction of policy, he found no reason to alter the framework the Federalists had erected.

By 1801 there were about 3,000 federal civilian employees in a nation of a little more than 5 million people. Growth in territory and population steadily enlarged national responsibilities. Thirty years later, when Jackson was president, there were more than 11,000 government workers in a nation of 13 million. The federal establishment was increasing at a faster rate than the population.

Jackson's presidency brought significant changes in the federal service. He believed that the executive branch contained too many officials who saw their jobs as "species of property" and as "a means of promoting individual interest." Against the idea of a permanent service based on life tenure, Jackson argued for the periodic redistribution of federal offices, contending that this was the democratic way and that official duties could be made "so plain and simple that men of intelligence may readily qualify themselves for their performance." He called this policy rotation-in-office. His opponents called it the spoils system.

In fact, partisan legend exaggerated the extent of Jackson's removals. More than 80 percent of federal officeholders retained their jobs. Jackson discharged no larger a proportion of government workers than Jefferson had done a generation earlier. But the rise in these years of mass political parties gave federal patronage new importance as a means of building the party and of rewarding activists. Jackson's successors were less restrained in the distribu-

8

tion of spoils. As the federal establishment grew—to nearly 40,000 by 1861—the politicization of the public service excited increasing concern.

After the Civil War the spoils system became a major political issue. High-minded men condemned it as the root of all political evil. The spoilsmen, said the British commentator James Bryce, "have distorted and depraved the mechanism of politics." Patronage, by giving jobs to unqualified, incompetent, and dishonest persons, lowered the standards of public service and nourished corrupt political machines. Office-seekers pursued presidents and cabinet secretaries without mercy. "Patronage," said Ulysses S. Grant after his presidency, "is the bane of the presidential office." "Every time I appoint someone to office," said another political leader, "I make a hundred enemies and one ingrate." George William Curtis, the president of the National Civil Service Reform League, summed up the indictment. He said,

> The theory which perverts public trusts into party spoils, making public employment dependent upon personal favor and not on proved merit, necessarily ruins the self-respect of public employees, destroys the function of party in a republic, prostitutes elections into a desperate strife for personal profit, and degrades the national character by lowering the moral tone and standard of the country.

The object of civil service reform was to promote efficiency and honesty in the public service and to bring about the ethical regeneration of public life. Over bitter opposition from politicians, the reformers in 1883 passed the Pendleton Act, establishing a bipartisan Civil Service Commission, competitive examinations, and appointment on merit. The Pendleton Act also gave the president authority to extend by executive order the number of "classified" jobs—that is, jobs subject to the merit system. The act applied initially only to about 14,000 of the more than 100,000 federal positions. But by the end of the 19th century 40 percent of federal jobs had moved into the classified category.

Civil service reform was in part a response to the growing complexity of American life. As society grew more organized and problems more technical, official duties were no longer so plain and simple that any person of intelligence could perform them. In public service, as in other areas, the all-round man was yielding ground to the expert, the amateur to the professional. The excesses of the spoils system thus provoked the counter-ideal of scientific public administration, separate from politics and, as far as possible, insulated against it.

The cult of the expert, however, had its own excesses. The idea that administration could be divorced from policy was an illusion. And in the realm of policy, the expert, however much segregated from partisan politics, can never attain perfect objectivity. He remains the prisoner of his own set of values. It is these values rather than technical expertise that determine fundamental judgments of public policy. To turn over such judgments to experts, moreover, would be to abandon democracy itself; for in a democracy final decisions must be made by the people and their elected representatives. "The business of the expert," the British political scientist Harold Laski rightly said, "is to be on tap and not on top."

Politics, however, were deeply ingrained in American folkways. This meant intermittent tension between the presidential government, elected every four years by the people, and the permanent government, which saw presidents come and go while it went on forever. Sometimes the permanent government knew better than its political masters; sometimes it opposed or sabotaged valuable new initiatives. In the end a strong president with effective cabinet secretaries could make the permanent government responsive to presidential purpose, but it was often an exasperating struggle.

The struggle within the executive branch was less important, however, than the growing impatience with bureaucracy in society as a whole. The 20th century saw a considerable expansion of the federal establishment. The Great Depression and the New Deal led the national government to take on a variety of new responsibilities. The New Deal extended the federal regulatory apparatus. By 1940, in a nation of 130 million people, the number of federal workers for the first time passed the 1 million mark. The Second World War brought federal civilian employment to 3.8 million in 1945. With peace, the federal establishment declined to around 2 million by 1950. Then growth resumed, reaching 2.8 million by the 1980s.

The New Deal years saw rising criticism of "big government" and "bureaucracy." Businessmen resented federal regulation. Conservatives worried about the impact of paternalistic government on individual self-reliance, on community responsibility, and on economic and personal freedom. The nation in effect renewed the old debate between Hamilton and Jefferson in the early republic, although with an ironic exchange of positions. For the Hamiltonian constituency, the "rich and well-born," once the advocate of affirmative government, now condemned government intervention, while the Jeffersonian constituency, the plain people, once the advocate of a weak central government and of states' rights, now favored government intervention.

In the 1980s, with the presidency of Ronald Reagan, the debate has burst out with unusual intensity. According to conservatives, government intervention abridges liberty, stifles enterprise, and is inefficient, wasteful, and arbitrary. It disturbs the harmony of the self-adjusting market and creates worse troubles than it solves. Get government off our backs, according to the popular cliché, and our problems will solve themselves. When government is necessary, let it be at the local level, close to the people. Above all, stop the inexorable growth of the federal government.

In fact, for all the talk about the "swollen" and "bloated" bureaucracy, the federal establishment has not been growing as inexorably as many Americans seem to believe. In 1949, it consisted of 2.1 million people. Thirty years later, while the country had grown by 70 million, the federal force had grown only by 750,000. Federal workers were a smaller percentage of the population in 1985 than they were in 1955—or in 1940. The federal establishment, in short, has not kept pace with population growth. Moreover, national defense and the postal service account for 60 percent of federal employment.

Why then the widespread idea about the remorseless growth of government? It is partly because in the 1960s the national government assumed new and intrusive functions: affirmative action in civil rights, environmental protection, safety and health in the workplace, community organization, legal aid to the poor. Although this enlargement of the federal regulatory role was accompanied by marked growth in the size of government on all levels, the expansion has taken place primarily in state and local government. Whereas the federal force increased by only 27 percent in the 30 years after 1950, the state and local government force increased by an astonishing 212 percent.

Despite the statistics, the conviction flourishes in some minds that the national government is a steadily growing behemoth swallowing up the liberties of the people. The foes of Washington prefer local government, feeling it is closer to the people and therefore allegedly more responsive to popular needs. Obviously there is a great deal to be said for settling local questions locally. But local government is characteristically the government of the locally powerful. Historically, the way the locally powerless have won their human and constitutional rights has often been through appeal to the national government. The national government has vindicated racial justice against local bigotry, defended the Bill of Rights against local vigilantism, and protected natural resources against local greed. It has civilized industry and secured the rights of labor organizations. Had the states' rights creed prevailed, there would perhaps still be slavery in the United States.

The national authority, far from diminishing the individual, has given most Americans more personal dignity and liberty than ever before. The individual freedoms destroyed by the increase in national authority have been in the main the freedom to deny black Americans their rights as citizens; the freedom to put small children to work in mills and immigrants in sweatshops; the freedom to pay starvation wages, require barbarous working hours, and permit squalid working conditions; the freedom to deceive in the sale of goods and securities; the freedom to pollute the environment—all freedoms that, one supposes, a civilized nation can readily do without.

"Statements are made," said President John F. Kennedy in 1963, "labelling the Federal Government an outsider, an intruder, an adversary. . . . The United States Government is not a stranger or not an enemy. It is the people of fifty states joining in a national effort. . . . Only a great national effort by a great people working together can explore the mysteries of space, harvest the products at the bottom of the ocean, and mobilize the human, natural, and material resources of our lands."

So an old debate continues. However, Americans are of two minds. When pollsters ask large, spacious questions—Do you think government has become too involved in your lives? Do you think government should stop regulating business?—a sizable majority opposes big government. But when asked specific questions about the practical work of government—Do you favor social security? unemployment compensation? Medicare? health and safety standards in factories? environmental protection? government guarantee of jobs for everyone seeking employment? price and wage controls when inflation threatens?—a sizable majority approves of intervention.

In general, Americans do not want less government. What they want is more efficient government. They want government to do a better job. For a time in the 1970s, with Vietnam and Watergate, Americans lost confidence in the national government. In 1964, more than three-quarters of those polled had thought the national government could be trusted to do right most of the time. By 1980 only one-quarter was prepared to offer such trust. But by 1984 trust in the federal government to manage national affairs had climbed back to 45 percent.

Bureaucracy is a term of abuse. But it is impossible to run any large organization, whether public or private, without a bureaucracy's division of labor and hierarchy of authority. And we live in a world of large organizations. Without bureaucracy modern society would collapse. The problem is not to abolish bureaucracy, but to make it flexible, efficient, and capable of innovation.

Two hundred years after the drafting of the Constitution, Americans still regard government with a mixture of reliance and mistrust—a good combination. Mistrust is the best way to keep government reliable. Informed criticism is the means of correcting governmental inefficiency, incompetence, and arbitrariness; that is, of best enabling government to play its essential role. For without government, we cannot attain the goals of the Founding Fathers. Without an understanding of government, we cannot have the informed criticism that makes government do the job right. It is the duty of every American citizen to know our government—which is what this series is all about.

In his inaugural speech, President John F. Kennedy urged young Americans to join the fight against worldwide poverty and ignorance. His message was to be embodied in the Peace Corps.

ONE

An Eloquent Challenge

On January 22, 1961, Washington, D.C., was covered with almost eight inches of new snow and buffeted by bitter winds and freezing temperatures. Shortly after noon on that cold and snowy day, John F. Kennedy took the oath of office as the 35th president of the United States. Standing on a dais in front of the Capitol, the new president issued a clarion call to the nation, exhorting Americans to "ask not what your country can do for you—ask what you can do for your country."

Kennedy, at 43 the youngest man ever elected president, challenged a "new generation of Americans" to join "a grand and global alliance" to fight tyranny, poverty, disease, and war. Speaking with a Boston accent in the 22-degree temperature, his head bare of the usual formal top hat, Kennedy used his eloquence and passion to introduce Americans to the idea that individuals could make a difference in the world. He told the audience that they could play a part in combating the ills that plagued the Third World—loosely, the underdeveloped countries of Africa, Asia, and Central and South America.

President Kennedy said that it would take "our best efforts to help them [the poor people in the developing nations] help themselves, for whatever period is required—not because the Communists may be doing it, not because we seek their votes, but because it is right. If a free society cannot help the many who are poor, it cannot save the few who are rich."

Marcia and Lance Haddon work with one of their neighbors to build an adobe wall around their house in Chirapaca, Bolivia, in 1968. Young Peace Corps volunteers, the Haddons embodied President Kennedy's desire to help developing nations and to promote international friendship.

Although the president never mentioned in his inaugural address exactly how Americans might contribute to easing the burdens of the poorer countries, he had a specific agenda in mind. Foremost in Kennedy's thoughts was the idea of harnessing American idealism and turning it into a program of good works known as the Peace Corps. He envisioned the Peace Corps as an agency that would send American volunteers to Third World nations. Working directly with villagers and townspeople, Peace Corps volunteers would initiate projects to help developing societies prosper and grow. At the same time, the corps would make a vital contribution to international understanding.

Kennedy established the Peace Corps by executive order in March 1961, and later that year Congress made the corps a permanent government agency. In line with the president's stirring challenge, Congress directed the Peace Corps to promote world peace and friendship by providing developing countries with skilled men and women. At the same time, Congress intended the corps to bring about mutual understanding between the people of the United States and those of developing nations.

Peace Corps volunteer Mike Sweet works in a well-improvement program in rural Yemen. The Peace Corps provides developing countries with workers skilled in a number of areas, including education, water-resource development, sanitation, health care, and agriculture.

Nutrition volunteer Christy Collins shops in a local market in Ayorou, Niger. In addition to providing valuable assistance to people in the Third World, Peace Corps volunteers learn about other cultures and discover unexpected strengths within themselves.

During the nearly three decades since its creation, the Peace Corps's goals have remained the same. The agency has lost some of the glamour and high visibility that made it so popular in Kennedy's time; what it has not lost, however, is its ability to quietly make a difference in people's lives in villages and towns around the world.

In 1988 the Peace Corps had approximately 6,000 volunteers in 65 nations in Latin America, Africa, Asia, and the Pacific Islands. Peace Corps volunteers offer valuable assistance in a wide variety of fields—including education, vocational training, maternal and child health care, nutrition, business start-up, forestry, conservation, engineering, and resource development. Each volunteer receives three months of intensive skill training, language instruction, and a cultural introduction to the host country. During the training period and two-year tour of duty, volunteers receive a monthly allowance for rent, food, travel, and medical needs. In addition to this allowance, a sum of $200 per month is set aside for every volunteer to receive upon completion of the 24-month service. This adds up to a nest egg of $4,800 at the end of the volunteer's tour of duty.

Though a nest egg is one rewarding finish to service as a Peace Corps volunteer, the real payment is in the adventure and discovery that many Americans experience as a result of their time in the Peace Corps. The adventure is in traveling to far-off lands, meeting new people, and learning about their culture and civilization. In addition to this learning process, many volunteers discover new strengths within themselves as they grow to meet the challenge of the Peace Corps.

One young volunteer who served in Colombia in the 1960s summed up the belief that motivates many of the men and women in the Peace Corps. In a letter written to his parents shortly before he died in a plane crash, David Crozier said, "Should it come to it, I had rather give my life trying to help someone than to have to give my life looking down a gun barrel at them."

Dr. Thomas Dooley (front right) poses with members of his hospital staff in Vang Vieng, Laos, in 1956. Dooley's belief in the importance of one-on-one aid, as opposed to traditional large-scale economic aid programs, greatly influenced the founders of the Peace Corps.

TWO

Armies of Peace

The Peace Corps was not an original idea. Long before the agency was established in 1961, religious groups, private organizations, and even governments were sending volunteers to less-developed regions to do charitable works. The United Nations Educational, Scientific, and Cultural Organization (UNESCO), a group formed in 1946 to promote peace and international understanding through education and research, estimates that at the time the Peace Corps was organized more than 300,000 volunteers from 41 countries were working in various projects in the Middle East, Africa, Asia, and Latin America.

The earliest volunteers who served as forerunners of the Peace Corps were religious missionaries. Beginning in the 16th century, Christian missionaries from Europe ventured as far as Africa, South America, Asia, and the South Pacific seeking converts to Christianity. By the 19th century, the missionary movement had gained enormous momentum, especially in Africa, where religious workers labored to stop the slave trade as well as to bring the Protestant and Catholic religions to what they saw as the continent's "heathen" population.

Approximately 10 million Africans were enslaved and forcibly taken to the New World between the 17th and 19th centuries. Many of these unlucky captives had been sold into slavery by rival tribes who cruelly profited from the slave trade.

Eighteenth-century Christian missionaries baptize native tribesmen in the Congo. Missionaries went to Africa to convert the native peoples to Christianity and to help curb the slave trade.

In the early 1800s, Thomas Fowell Buxton, a founder of the Christian Missionary Society in London, preached that the slave trade could be rooted out by developing agriculture and commerce in Africa. The new trade, Buxton thought, would replace slave trading, making it economically unprofitable for Africans to sell other Africans into slavery. He described the role of religious workers in this process: "Let missionaries and schoolmasters, the plough and the spade, go together and agriculture will flourish; the avenues to legitimate commerce will be opened."

Buxton convinced the British government to sponsor an expedition to West Africa to begin the work of bringing prosperity to the continent. Plans for the expedition read like a blueprint worthy of a Peace Corps development program: Government agents, scientists, doctors, farmers, traders, and missionaries were to sail on three steamships up a major African waterway, the Niger River in West Africa, in what is now called Nigeria. They were to locate sites for schools, missions, and model farms and to study the possibilities that existed in the region for trade and commerce.

The expedition set sail in the spring of 1841 and by early fall had reached the river's delta and turned upstream. Then, many of the passengers were struck by malaria, a tropical disease that is transmitted by mosquitoes. Malaria causes bouts of sweating, shivering, and, eventually, delirium; in the mid-1800s there was no known cure, and the disease was often fatal.

Within two months, all three steamships had been forced to turn back because of the malaria outbreak. At first it seemed as if the Niger expedition, which had started out with high hopes, had turned into a complete disaster. Fortunately, though, the ideas generated by the expedition lived on, and future missionaries set out to accomplish Buxton's goal of social, educational, and commercial development of the continent.

Later missionaries built on Buxton's model by establishing hospitals, pioneering the study of native languages, and fostering trade, education, and industry throughout Africa. Promoting education was the missionaries' greatest achievement; in fact, many of the African leaders who led their countries to independence from colonial rule after World War II—including Jomo Kenyatta

President Julius Nyerere of Tanzania meets with Peace Corps director Jack Hood Vaughn in 1966. Like many 20th-century African leaders, Nyerere was educated in a mission school.

23

of Kenya, Julius Nyerere of Tanzania, and Kenneth Kaunda of Zambia—were educated in missionary schools.

By 1961, the year the Peace Corps was established, more than 400 different Protestant and Catholic organizations had a total of 33,000 missionaries in developing countries around the world. Groups such as the National Lutheran Council, Church World Service, and the Quaker-affiliated American Friends Service Committee sent volunteers to African, Asian, and South American countries every year to work in hospitals, schools, and other service projects. By going on missions to less-developed countries and working closely with local people to improve the quality of life, these Christian missionaries served as models for the Peace Corps volunteers.

The "First Peace Corps"

The modern Peace Corps is also descended from a turn-of-the-century U.S. government program of reconstruction and rehabilitation in the Philippines that is popularly known as the "First Peace Corps."

The United States gained control of the Philippines in 1899, after winning the Spanish-American War. It had declared war on Spain primarily to win independence for the island of Cuba, but victory also brought the United States control of the Spanish colonies of Puerto Rico, Guam, and the Philippines. While putting down a postwar Filipino rebellion, American soldiers destroyed much of the Philippine islands. When peace came in 1902, the United States began rebuilding what had been destroyed. The U.S. program also sent doctors to fight disease, teachers to work in village schools, and nutrition experts to research cures for native diet-deficiency diseases.

In 1905 the U.S. government established a civilian department of health in the islands and named Dr. Victor Heiser, an expert in tropical diseases, to head the new agency. Heiser and his staff eliminated the causes of many infectious diseases by arranging for garbage and sewage disposal, purifying the drinking water, and vaccinating the population against smallpox and other diseases. Heiser also established a colony to house victims of leprosy, an infectious disease that can lead to disfigurement and the loss of limbs.

Another disease prevalent in the islands at that time was beriberi. The U.S. Army sent Robert R. Williams, an organic chemist, to work on conquering this disease, which can lead to paralysis, emaciation, heart failure, and death. At the time, beriberi killed about 25,000 people annually in the Philippines. Williams concluded that the Filipino diet, which was largely based on rice, was

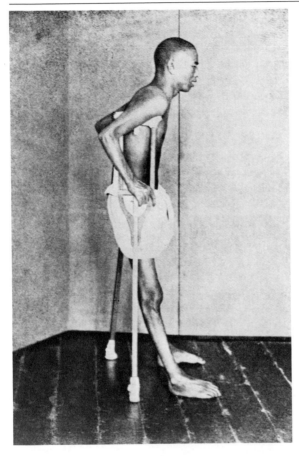

An emaciated beriberi victim. Chemist Robert R. Williams discovered a cure for this potentially fatal disease while working in the Philippines at the turn of the century under a U.S. government program known as the "First Peace Corps."

the cause of the disease's prevalence: The Filipinos processed (or polished) rice, rather than consuming unmilled brown rice, and thus they washed away important vitamins that prevented beriberi.

Williams made up a solution from the extract of the rice-polishings and would often rush to the *barrios*, or neighborhoods, to treat children suffering from the disease. Several hours after drinking a few drops of this solution, the children would begin to recover. Twenty-six years later, Williams discovered the key ingredient in the extract—vitamin B_1, or thiamine.

U.S. government aid improved the lives of the Filipino people through education as well. When the war ended, many young soldiers had decided to stay in the Philippines and teach English in the small barrio schools. Their numbers were later augmented by hundreds of other young volunteer teachers sent by the U.S. Department of the Interior. The islanders came to respect these men and women because of their willingness to teach in cramped, one-room schoolhouses in isolated villages and to live with the local people in the barrios. By 1926 the program was such a success that the percentage of people in the Philippines with a high school education was greater than in more-developed countries such as Sweden or Spain.

International Voluntary Services

While government foreign-aid efforts continued to help needy nations, the private sector was also working to alleviate Third World poverty. One private organization that served as a model for the modern Peace Corps was the International Voluntary Services (IVS), formed in 1953 as an outgrowth of

International Voluntary Services worker Rudy Vigil works with an Algerian woman on a water-resource development project in the 1960s. The IVS's founders created the person-to-person aid organization in 1953 to counter America's negative image abroad.

American missionary work. Although this group was composed of Catholic and Protestant representatives, it had no religious agenda and was purely a service organization. Between 1953 and 1961, the IVS sent about 200 people to work overseas.

Many people in the mission societies charged that U.S. foreign-aid programs were not reaching remote, impoverished towns and villages. They formed the IVS to remedy this problem. They also hoped to improve the image of the United States abroad. After World War II, in the late 1940s and 1950s, many foreigners viewed the United States as a rich, industrialized "big brother." They admired the wealth and power of America, but, at the same time, they resented it. From 1948 to 1952, under the Marshall Plan, the U.S. government sent more than $12 billion in aid to 16 Western European countries devastated by the war. The government would later send money to many newly emerging nations. International resentment of U.S. wealth and power came to be symbolized in the image of the "ugly American"—a rich, brash fellow who smoked fat cigars and flaunted his wealth and power in the face of poorer people in foreign countries. (The phrase was taken from *The Ugly American*, a 1958 novel written by Eugene Burdick and William Lederer in which American diplomats live a rich, privileged life overseas, in contrast to the poverty surrounding them.)

The IVS tried to counter these anti-American sentiments by working one-on-one in the towns and villages of developing countries. In contrast to typical U.S. aid projects, such as dam or highway construction, IVS volunteers concentrated primarily on small agricultural projects throughout the Middle East, Asia, and Africa. With little fanfare or publicity they cleared jungles, grew experimental crops, dug wells, raised poultry, and in turn made a significant impact on the lives of individual villagers. IVS projects and the volunteers who carried them out proved invaluable to the developing countries. For example, when a conflict over the Suez Canal in Egypt broke out in 1956, 2 young IVS volunteers who were running a 33-acre experimental farm nearby were evacuated; when a truce was declared, the Egyptian government immediately asked for the return of the volunteers.

Dr. Tom Dooley

Another important model for the first Peace Corps volunteers was Thomas Dooley, a U.S. Navy doctor who served in Vietnam. Formerly a French colony, the Indochinese country had gained its independence in 1954 after a fierce eight-year war and was partitioned into a communist-run north and a pro-West south. In 1953, near the end of the conflict, Dooley established large refugee camps at Haiphong, North Vietnam, to house, feed, and provide medical care to the thousands of refugees who were waiting for U.S. ships to transport them to Saigon in South Vietnam. The disease and poverty of these Asians made an indelible impression on Dooley, and he resolved to return to Southeast Asia after the war's conclusion.

When his tour of duty in the navy was completed, Dooley organized a medical mission under the aegis of the International Rescue Committee (IRC), a humanitarian organization dedicated to helping refugees. Dooley and three of his former navy medical corpsmen raised money to establish a small hospital in Laos, a landlocked kingdom in the middle of the Indochina peninsula. He chose Laos primarily because other organizations were already helping in South Vietnam and he preferred to serve where the need was most critical. In 1956, Laos, a country of 2 million people, had only 1 doctor.

By this time, Dooley was an American folk hero. In addition to writing numerous newspaper articles, giving lectures, and making television appearances, he had written a popular book on his experiences in Vietnam, called *Deliver Us From Evil*. Private donations for his medical mission were supplemented by U.S. companies such as Pfizer and Johnson & Johnson, pharmaceutical firms that donated thousands of dollars in antibiotics, bandages, dressings, surgical instruments, vitamins, protein supplements, and a jeep. Film mogul Walt Disney even contributed a sound projector and a collection of Disney movies.

In 1956, Dooley set up a hospital in the village of Vang Vieng, Laos, in a whitewashed building with three rooms. He and his three co-workers lived nearby in a typical Laotian two-room hut perched six feet above the ground on stout poles. Dooley recalled, "We never announced sick-call and we needed no publicity. Only a few days after our arrival, we were awakened one morning by sounds that were to become a familiar part of every dawn—the howls of sickly babies, the hacking coughs of tubercular mothers." Besides treating patients, the team trained nurses and midwives and gave courses in public health and nutrition to villagers.

Although everyone knew he was an American doctor, Dooley wrote that his philosophy was not to preach or extol the virtues of democracy or of the United States. He was critical of most U.S. government medical programs, calling them more "dollar to person than person to person." He believed that volunteers should live with villagers, even if it meant staying in a hut on stilts.

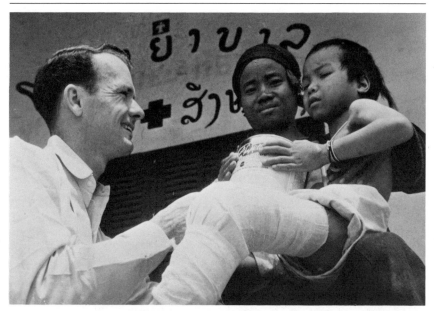

Dr. Thomas Dooley (left) believed that aid teams should live among the people they were helping. After establishing a much-needed hospital in Laos in 1956, he founded MEDICO, an organization that sent volunteer medical teams to impoverished areas around the world.

At the time of Dooley's death from cancer in 1961, 94 doctors were working for the organization he established, MEDICO (Medical International Cooperation). The group sent medical teams to countries around the world, including Cambodia, Laos, Malaya (which was incorporated into the Federation of Malaysia in 1963), Haiti, Jordan, Peru, and Afghanistan. Explaining his mission, Dooley had said that he and his fellow workers "wanted eloquence in deeds, not words." The success of this philosophy and of Dooley's belief in the need for personal involvement in aid programs heavily influenced the framers of the Peace Corps.

Aid Programs at Home

In addition to its overseas aid programs, the United States organized young men and women to work on development projects within its own borders. President Franklin D. Roosevelt, elected in 1932 during the Great Depression,

A National Youth Administration crew loads tree branches into a truck. Established in 1935, the NYA provided employment to 5 million young people during the Great Depression.

believed that the talents and idealism of America's youth could be harnessed and directed into constructive areas. His New Deal, a program of relief and recovery from the economic catastrophe of the depression, was based in part upon this philosophy.

In 1933, Roosevelt created the Civilian Conservation Corps (CCC), a New Deal program designed to channel the energy of 2 million young men who were unable to find employment during the depression. CCC workers did much of the backbreaking work that developed the country's system of national parks: They planted trees and built roads, buildings, picnic facilities, and dams. In 1935, Roosevelt established the National Youth Administration (NYA), a federal agency that hired about 5 million unemployed young people and students to do everything from clearing swamps and building schools and hospitals to teaching illiterate adults how to read.

Congressional Enthusiasm for a Peace Corps

By the late 1950s, successful aid programs in developing countries, Roosevelt's example of a youth corps, and the desire to change the image of the "ugly American" had convinced some American legislators of the promise of a government-sponsored, voluntary "army for peace." Democratic congressman Henry Reuss of Wisconsin described this new foreign-aid philosophy in a statement in *Commonweal* magazine that he wrote after returning from a trip to Cambodia in 1957. Like Vietnam, Cambodia had been a French colony. Although the country had won its independence in 1953, it remained war torn and impoverished.

Reuss's trip started him thinking about foreign-aid programs that would affect life at the village level. He wrote,

> Too often we seem to emphasize military alliances with corrupt or reactionary leaders; furnishing military hardware which all too frequently is turned on the people of the country we are presumably helping; grandiose and massive projects; hordes of American officials living aloof in the country's capital. Would we not be farther along if we relied more heavily on a group of some thousands of young Americans willing to help with an irrigation project, digging a village well, or setting up a rural school?

Reuss told how he had driven along an impressive new highway built with $30 million of U.S. foreign aid. The highway was empty except for a barefoot Cambodian leading his water buffalo along the side of the road. Reuss asked himself, "How else might we have spent that money to serve more people?"

Later in his trip, Reuss met a team of four young American schoolteachers in a village in the Cambodian jungle. Working under the auspices of UNESCO, they were going from village to village setting up elementary schools. Reuss noted that the villagers and the Americans were drawn to one another, and he regretted that there were only 4, rather than 40 or 400, Americans working on this project.

Reuss became so enamored of the idea of young volunteers serving abroad that he proposed that the government establish a group called the Point Four Youth Corps. He derived the name from former president Harry S. Truman's 1949 Point Four program—named after the fourth point of Truman's inaugural address—which offered technical assistance to developing countries. In 1960, Reuss submitted a bill to the House of Representatives requesting funds for a

31

Senator Hubert Humphrey (right) poses with John F. Kennedy. Humphrey provided the Peace Corps with strong congressional support.

study of his proposal. Congress approved the bill and made available $10,000. The study, conducted by the University of Colorado Research Foundation in Boulder, was presented to President Kennedy in 1961 and formed much of the basis for the Peace Corps.

Another legislator impressed with the idea of a youth corps was Democratic senator Hubert Humphrey of Minnesota, who later served as vice-president under Lyndon B. Johnson from 1965 to 1969. In 1960 the senator submitted a bill that went further than the Reuss legislation, bypassing a study and asking for the establishment of a "peace corps" modeled after the IVS. Senator Humphrey believed that a youth corps could serve two purposes: First, the young volunteers would offer worthwhile aid; and second, the corps would serve as a recruiting ground for government agencies such as the Foreign Service, which staffs U.S. embassies overseas with diplomatic officers.

"There is nothing which will build greater people-to-people and government-to-government relationships than to have fine young American men helping the people of the emerging countries to help themselves," the senator later wrote in a book about the Peace Corps. "They will not only act as instructors but also will show that they are not afraid to dirty their hands in their common endeavors." Although the Humphrey proposal was introduced too late in the

32

1960 legislative session to be acted upon, it did help to stimulate public interest in overseas volunteerism.

Early in 1960 the peace corps concept was brought to the attention of Democratic senator John F. Kennedy as he waged his campaign for the presidency. During a television panel show with college students, Kennedy was asked how he felt about the Reuss proposal. Kennedy responded that he was unfamiliar with the bill but favored the concept. He later asked staffers to research the proposal and, impressed by the idea's popularity, eventually adopted it as part of his campaign platform. Thereafter, although the Peace Corps had many framers, it became forever entwined with the youthful idealism and spirit of John F. Kennedy.

The Kennedy Campaign

At 2:00 A.M. one chilly October morning in 1960, Senator Kennedy made a campaign stop on the campus of the University of Michigan in Ann Arbor. He had just completed his third televised debate with his challenger, Vice-

Senator John F. Kennedy's 2:00 A.M. campaign speech at the University of Michigan in 1960 sparked an interest in overseas voluntary service. Soon afterward, he formally added the Peace Corps to his campaign platform.

33

president Richard Nixon, and he was exhausted from the debate and the late-night flight from New York. When he reached the campus and saw the crowd waiting he agreed to speak, although he had no prepared text. Standing on the steps of the student union building, surrounded by 10,000 noisy students, his voice hoarse from campaigning, Kennedy challenged the audience:

> How many of you are willing to spend ten years in Africa or Latin America or Asia working for the U.S. and working for freedom? How many of you [who] are going to be doctors are willing to spend your days in Ghana; technicians or engineers, how many of you are willing to work in the foreign service, and spend your lives traveling around the world?

Kennedy's impromptu question was eagerly answered by students on college campuses around the country. They organized groups favoring overseas service, signed petitions, and flooded the Kennedy campaign and the Democratic national headquarters with enthusiastic mail. One student who had heard Kennedy speak at the University of Michigan wrote about that night, "The message he left behind was that young people could make a difference in helping to create a better and more peaceful world. He told us we had skills that were useful and ideals that could serve the future of our country. We responded."

Not everyone supported the concept of a peace corps, however. One newspaper columnist mockingly called it the "Kiddie Korps," and Richard Nixon labeled the corps "a haven for draft dodgers." Because the Humphrey plan called for exempting peace corps participants from the military draft—which, until it was abolished in 1973, required every able-bodied American male 18 or older to serve 2 years in the U.S. military—Nixon charged that candidates for peace corps work could easily use the corps as an excuse to avoid such service. Because of Nixon's criticism, later peace corps proposals asked instead for a military deferment.

Such attacks, however, did not reflect most Americans' reception of the peace corps proposal: A Gallup poll conducted in January 1961 showed that 71 percent of U.S. citizens favored a peace corps, whereas only 18 percent opposed it.

In September 1960, before a crowd of about 40,000 in San Francisco, California, Kennedy signaled his formal commitment to the idea of a peace corps, broadening the Reuss and Humphrey proposals by adding women and older Americans as candidates for such a program. Kennedy said,

34

We are going to have to have the best Americans we can get to speak for our country abroad. . . . All of us have admired what Dr. Tom Dooley has done in Laos. And others have been discouraged at the examples that we read of the ugly American. And I think that the United States is going to have to do much better in this area if we are going to defend freedom and peace in the 1960s.

Kennedy's Streams of Interest

After Kennedy assumed the presidency in January 1961, pressure to establish a peace corps intensified. The new president's press secretary, Pierre Salinger, reported that Kennedy had received more mail on that subject than on any other campaign issue. Such mail continued to pour into the White House. It became apparent that this proposal had strong support among Americans, particularly college students, and that the enthusiasm it had generated was not just campaign fever.

Theodore Sorensen, the new president's special counsel and later one of his biographers, explained that the idea of an army for peace fit Kennedy's personal and political sympathies. He described the Peace Corps as a "lake" into which several of the president's "streams of interest" flowed.

One stream of interest was President Kennedy's deep concern about the deficiencies of Third World societies. Kennedy had traveled extensively in Europe, Asia, and Latin America and had seen firsthand the poverty and disease rampant in many underdeveloped countries. He wanted to forge a new relationship between the United States and developing nations, based on respect and political understanding, to help those countries prosper. The Peace Corps was a key part of that new relationship. (Kennedy also established the Alliance for Progress, a $100 billion social- and economic-development program for Latin American countries, at this time.)

A second stream that contributed to Kennedy's enthusiasm for the Peace Corps was his desire to revitalize the government's foreign-assistance programs. He had long been critical of what he perceived as U.S. insensitivity to the needs of developing countries. Kennedy had also objected to the Republican party's concentration on military aid at the expense of social- and economic-development programs in impoverished Third World nations. In San Francisco, Kennedy told his audience that "Men who lack compassion . . . were sent abroad to represent us in countries which were marked by disease and poverty and illiteracy and ignorance, and they did not identify us with those causes and the fight against them." Kennedy believed that technical assistance and

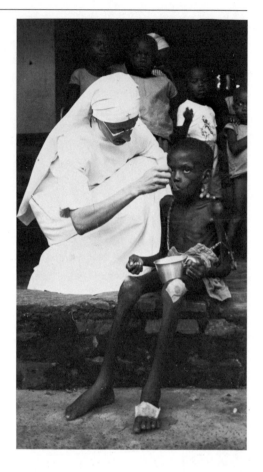

An American nun feeds a starving child at a hospital in the Congo in 1960. President Kennedy, who had observed similar conditions in many Third World countries, was eager to establish the Peace Corps to contribute to such aid efforts.

education projects should be the mainstay of American foreign-assistance programs: "Our aid now should be concentrated not on large-scale monuments to American engineering but on the village and the farm."

Kennedy also strongly believed in sharing the democratic ideals of the United States with Third World countries. At the time, the United States was locked in a nonmilitary struggle with the Soviet Union called the cold war, which pitted the American capitalist, free-enterprise system (based on private ownership of property and the means of production) against the Soviets' communist form of government. The two superpowers were fighting for the hearts and minds of the Third World. President Kennedy saw in the Peace Corps a way to combat the Soviet influence in Third World countries and win this ideological war.

Executive Order 10924

President Kennedy was eager to put the Peace Corps into action. Soon after taking office, he appointed R. Sargent Shriver, his brother-in-law, to study whether the corps could be organized and started immediately. Shriver, a lawyer, journalist, and businessman, had long been interested in student projects. While an undergraduate at Yale in the late 1930s, he had led student groups to Europe to study the culture and live with local families. After serving in the U.S. Navy in World War II, he was hired by the Kennedy family to run business interests in Chicago. In 1953 he married John Kennedy's sister Eunice.

Shriver read the various reports that had been prepared for the new president, as well as the Reuss and Humphrey proposals. By the end of February, he made his recommendation to Kennedy: The "Peace Corps should be launched soon so that the opportunity to recruit the most qualified people from this year's graduating classes will not be lost. Nor should we lose the opportunity to use this summer for training on university campuses."

On March 1, 1961, two days after receiving Shriver's recommendation and less than two months after taking office, the president issued Executive Order 10924, establishing the Peace Corps as a new agency within the Department of State. The executive order was sufficient to create the agency and start it functioning; however, Kennedy knew that congressional approval would be required to establish the corps as a permanent agency and provide for its funding. He sent a message to Congress explaining his executive order and recommending the permanent adoption of the proposal. He described the Peace Corps as "a pool of trained American men and women sent overseas by the U.S. Government or through private organizations and institutions to help foreign countries meet their urgent needs for skilled manpower." A few days later, Kennedy officially appointed Sargent Shriver as the first director of the Peace Corps.

President Kennedy hands his pen to a pleased Sargent Shriver after signing the Peace Corps Act into law on September 22, 1961. Both men hailed the voluntary organization as a way to help bring about world peace.

THREE

A Triumphal
Beginning

Within days of his appointment, Shriver was engulfed in a whirlwind of activity, assembling a staff, setting up offices in Washington, D.C., and establishing procedures for the new agency. Observers described the first days of the Peace Corps as hectic, with telephones ringing, mail piling up on desks, and workmen moving office furniture. At the same time, requests for information and applications were inundating the agency staff, the White House, and congressional offices.

Shriver was determined from the outset that the Peace Corps not resemble a typical government agency—frequently mired in bureaucracy and red tape, slow to act, cautious, and stodgy. He wanted the corps to be dynamic and creative and able to inspire enthusiasm and dedication in its staff. To create this unique agency—what his staffers termed an "anti-bureaucratic bureaucracy"— Shriver focused first on hiring the right men and women to build the agency from the ground up. He believed that a specially talented staff was crucial to turning the Peace Corps into a reality quickly and efficiently.

One of Shriver's first choices was 34-year-old Harris Wofford, a law professor from Notre Dame University who had served as Kennedy's adviser on civil rights during the campaign. Wofford assumed a critical role as liaison between the White House and the new agency. Two others Shriver invited to join the corps were Warren Wiggins and William Josephson, both of whom had

During the early days of the Peace Corps, the agency's staff was forced to improvise with sketchy plans and a minimum of furniture and office supplies. Despite the apparent lack of organization, the corps's founders were busily working to establish it as a permanent government agency.

worked with President Eisenhower's foreign-aid agency, the International Cooperation Administration. (In Kennedy's administration the ICA was absorbed into a new foreign-aid unit called the Agency for International Development—AID.) These two young men had expressed dissatisfaction with the manner of foreign aid under the Eisenhower administration. Wiggins charged that U.S. officials living in Third World countries resided in "golden ghettos," removed from the poverty and hunger surrounding them. Wiggins took on the task of planning and developing overseas programs for Peace Corps volunteers. Josephson began drafting legislation to gain formal approval from Congress for the Peace Corps. Another new staff member was 26-year-old Bill Moyers, who had gained recognition for his work as Senator (now Vice-president) Lyndon B. Johnson's personal assistant. In two years, Moyers would be named deputy director of the Peace Corps—the youngest person ever to hold such a high official position in American government.

The Towering Task

Shriver, Wofford, Wiggins, Josephson, and Moyers served as the master builders of the new agency, relying on a position paper Wiggins and Josephson had drafted for the new president in the transition period between the November election and the January inauguration. Their report, called "The Towering Task," established a "quick start" philosophy that would govern the first years of the Peace Corps.

The report warned against the cautious "go slow" approach that had been urged by many government advisers. Instead, it called for a rapid start for the new agency, with "several thousand Americans participating in the first 12 to 18 months." Wiggins told a Peace Corps task force meeting in February 1961 that "a small cautious Peace Corps may be worse than no Peace Corps at all.

Harris Wofford (right) inspects a volunteer project in Ethiopia in the 1960s. One of the Peace Corps's master builders, Wofford served as director of the agency's Ethiopian program from 1962 to 1964 and as associate director of the corps from 1964 to 1966.

41

It may not receive the attention and talent it will require even for preventing trouble." He theorized that the new agency would need many participants in order to attract the publicity and acclaim that would keep qualified Americans applying. A larger number of volunteers would also enable the corps to help more people in each Third World country. Moreover, if one project did not work out, its failure would be overshadowed by many other successful projects.

The five men set a furious pace, working late into the night to organize the new agency. Shriver held many long and intense meetings with his staff to hammer out policy. At many of these often noisy discussions, Shriver would tear apart, enlarge, and recreate ideas so that the staff would joke that the original concept had been "Shriverized." One young man described the director's charisma by recalling that some agency staffers used to come in early in the morning just to wait and ride up in the elevator with Sarge, as they affectionately called him.

Skepticism at Home and Abroad

With the Peace Corps quickly becoming a reality, Shriver turned to his next priority: ensuring that the agency retain its independence within the Department of State. Soon after President Kennedy established the corps, officials within the vast federal foreign-aid bureaucracy criticized the degree of autonomy he had given the new agency. Many foreign-policy professionals opposed the idea of placing inexperienced young Americans in sensitive, newly emerging Third World nations. One career diplomat jibed at the idealistic Peace Corps volunteers, saying they wanted to "wreak some good on the natives."

Seeking to preserve the agency's upbeat, positive image and energetic style, Shriver and his staff argued that tying the Peace Corps to established foreign-aid programs would kill its esprit de corps, that special feeling that bound staffers to the new agency. Shriver also wanted the corps to present a separate identity to the American public and the governments of Third World nations. Many countries in Africa and Asia, newly freed from colonial rule, believed that traditional foreign-aid programs were imperialistic—an attempt by the United States to gain control of the new nations.

Despite opposition from some members of the foreign-policy establishment, the agency did have the support of the head of the Kennedy foreign-policy staff, Secretary of State Dean Rusk, and his under secretary of state, Chester Bowles. But the major figure who helped win the day for the Peace Corps was

Peace Corps director Sargent Shriver held numerous and lengthy staff meet-
ings to establish policies and procedures for the unique voluntary agency.
Young staffers were impressed by the director's drive and charisma.

Vice-president Lyndon B. Johnson. Asked by Moyers, his former staffer, to
help the new agency, the vice-president argued strongly for an independent
corps: "You put the Peace Corps into the foreign service and they'll put striped
pants on your people when all you want them to have is a knapsack and a tool
kit and a lot of imagination," Johnson told Moyers. "And they'll give you a
hundred and one reasons why it won't work every time you want to do
something different." He later convinced Kennedy to make the corps a
separate, semiautonomous unit with its director reporting to the secretary of
state.

In addition to skepticism on the home front, many foreign leaders and
government officials from countries such as India, Pakistan, Turkey, Mali, and
Burma openly expressed doubt that the Peace Corps could accomplish much
good. Others, such as President Kwame Nkrumah of Ghana, a leading
spokesman for African independence, feared that the Peace Corps might be a
means for the U.S. Central Intelligence Agency to spy on other countries.

To counter these negative images, Shriver set out on the first of many trips
abroad, traveling from capital to capital to inspire support for his Peace Corps

43

Sargent Shriver inspects a length of cloth at a bazaar in Katmandu, Nepal. The Peace Corps director made a number of overseas journeys to gain international support for the new agency.

volunteers. In a month's time he had returned to Washington with invitations from Ghana, Nigeria, Pakistan, India, Burma, Malaya, and the Philippines for a total of 3,000 Peace Corps workers. Within a few weeks, requests for volunteers came in from another 24 Third World nations.

In July, less than six months after Kennedy took the oath of office, the new agency announced that projects had been developed for Ghana, Tanzania, Colombia, the Philippines, Chile, and St. Lucia and that more than 5,000 applicants had taken the first exams to enter the Peace Corps. The corps was no longer just an idea or the subject of a task force or report; it had become a reality—a functioning agency with real participants and real goals.

The Peace Corps Act

It took several months for Congress to begin discussion of the bill to create the Peace Corps. At the end of May 1961 the president sent the Peace Corps Act to Congress, where it was introduced by Senator Humphrey and other interested legislators in the Senate and the House, including Congressman Reuss. The final bill passed Congress with an impressive majority and gave the Peace Corps $30 million in funding for 1962. On September 22, 1961, President Kennedy signed the bill into law and established the Peace Corps as a permanent agency within the Department of State.

The Peace Corps at Work

The new agency was divided into three sections: the headquarters staff, who recruited and trained volunteers and organized their projects; the Peace Corps representatives, who directed operations in particular countries or regions; and the Peace Corps volunteers themselves, who went out into the villages and towns and did the actual fieldwork.

Shriver devised several strategies to keep the Peace Corps fresh and functioning effectively. Under his leadership, the agency never published a formal policy manual, and every policy directive was labeled "interim"— meaning that it was subject to change. Shriver insisted that guidelines be flexible and ready to be modified as conditions changed within individual countries. An example of that flexibility at work occurred after a coup in the Dominican Republic in 1963. Ordinarily, U.S. citizens are evacuated from a country after an overthrow of a legitimate government. However, the Peace Corps representative in that country decided that the volunteers were in no danger and should not be removed. The agency maintained its relationship with the new regime, and shortly afterward the United States recognized the new government.

Another way Shriver kept the agency dynamic was by limiting headquarters staff. In the first 3 years of the corps's existence, there were 10 volunteers in the field for every staffer back in Washington. This compared favorably with other U.S. foreign-aid programs, which had a ratio of four people abroad for every person in Washington. Also helpful was the critical look the agency took at itself. A tough evaluation division sent lone inspectors or teams to visit each Peace Corps foreign operation. Through intensive interviewing and on-site

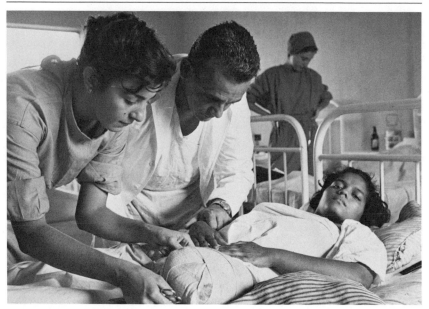

Peace Corps nurse Arleen Serino tends a woman wounded by an exploding mortar shell during the civil war that followed a 1963 coup in the Dominican Republic. Despite the political unrest, Peace Corps volunteers in that country remained at their posts.

inspection, the division judged the effectiveness of the particular project. This unit soon became the conscience of the Peace Corps.

Finally, Shriver set down a "no-career" philosophy for the Peace Corps. He stressed that the corps was a service, and that staffers should not make it a career. A 1963 memo, "In, Up and Out—A Plan to Keep the Peace Corps Permanently Young, Creative and Dynamic," suggested that all professional-level personnel be limited to five years of service. Shriver theorized that although talented staff would be lost, the infusion of new, enthusiastic personnel would constantly revitalize the corps. Congress enacted this policy into law in October 1965.

Successes and Trials

The first group of volunteers left for Africa in August 1961 after a presidential reception in the Rose Garden of the White House. Kennedy called the group, whose members were bound for road-surveying projects in Tanzania and teaching positions in Ghana, "a special group of young Americans." As he shook their hands and sent them off, he cautioned them that the world would be watching them: "There are of course a great many hundreds of millions of people scattered throughout the world. You will come in contact with only a few, but the great impression of what kind of country we have and what kind of people we are will depend on their judgement . . . of you."

The 51 Americans who landed in Accra, Ghana, made an immediate, positive impression upon their hosts. They formed a chorus on the airport's tarmac in front of the minister of education and other officials and began singing the Ghanaian national anthem in Twi, the local language. The officials were surprised and very pleased, and Radio Ghana played a tape of the performance many times.

Not everything went as smoothly or as positively as this auspicious beginning. Brent Ashabranner, the first Peace Corps administrator in Nigeria, recalled that the early race to put volunteers into the field occasionally backfired. Sometimes, he said, host-country officials did not know exactly who the volunteers were or what they were supposed to do. Sometimes, there were too many volunteers and too few assignments; promised living quarters

President Kennedy hails the first group of departing volunteers in the Rose Garden in August 1961. "We put a good deal of hope in the work that you do," the president told the early recruits.

turned out to be a foundation and no building; or training proved to be inadequate to the circumstances. But Ashabranner concluded that many of the lessons to be learned had to be a matter of trial and error and that no amount of planning could have foreseen everything.

The first event that shook the Peace Corps to its foundations occurred in October 1961 and involved a simple postcard. Margery Michelmore, a 23-year-old magna cum laude graduate of Smith College, was completing her Peace Corps training at the University College of Ibadan in Nigeria. Michelmore lost a postcard she had written to a friend in the United States describing the squalor and primitive living conditions all around her—people living, cooking, and peddling their wares in the streets, even relieving themselves in public. Someone picked up the postcard, and within hours it had been copied and distributed around campus.

Volunteer Peter Corey washes glasses in the courtyard outside his apartment in a slum in Santo Domingo, Dominican Republic, in 1966. The Peace Corps intended for volunteers to live among the people they helped, but the agency was sometimes unable to ensure that living quarters were adequate.

Dear Bobto - Don't be furious at getting a postcard. I promise a letter next time. I wanted you to see the incredible + fascinating city we were in. With all the training we had had, we really were not prepared for the squalor + absolutely primitive living conditions rampant both in the city + the bush. We had no idea about what "underdeveloped" meant. It really is a revelation + once we got over the initial horrified shock, a very rewarding experience. Everyone lives in the street — cooks in the street, sells in the street + even goes to the bathroom in the street. The university is great fun as it is something to be a foreign student anyway + especially to be the only white students in an all-African university. I just hope that they don't repeat last year's Lumumba riots. Please write. — Marg

We are excessively cut off from the rest of the world

*Queen Elizabeth Hall
University College
Ibadan, Nyjeria*

Robert V. Storer
89 Rice Street
Cambridge 40 Mass.
U.S.A

Margery Michelmore's October 1961 postcard to a friend in America caused a scandal that threatened future Peace Corps operations both in Nigeria and around the world. Nigerian students took offense at Michelmore's commentary on the poverty she saw in the city of Ibadan.

The Nigerian students reacted violently. Small riots broke out in the men's residence hall, and groups of students roamed the campus yelling, "Yankee go home!" and "Imperialist agents unwelcome!" Peace Corps trainees were banned from the student union, where they had previously enjoyed sodas and conversation with the local students. The trainees were quickly isolated. Meanwhile, the story had broken on the wire services and the news had spread around the world. Michelmore, heartbroken at causing such an incident, wrote an open letter apologizing for the postcard and its seemingly insensitive criticisms of Nigerian society. She returned to Washington to work at the Peace Corps headquarters and then went home to Massachusetts.

This unfortunate incident gave ammunition to the Peace Corps's critics. Former president Eisenhower, who had characterized the agency as an unsound idea, mocked the corps's mission: He suggested that the volunteers be sent to the moon, an underdeveloped "country" where they could do no harm.

However, the postcard episode had positive effects as well. It became legend within the corps, a classic case used to teach future volunteers about the sensitivities of Third World countries. Many among the American press took a supportive posture and from then on watched the Peace Corps closely to see how it would fare; fortunately, the majority of news articles were positive, and the corps continued to be warmly received at home. Nigerian students began talking to the trainees, and many frank discussions ensued about the motives of the volunteers and the goals of the corps. Additional volunteers arriving in Nigeria to take up posts were greeted without incident. They were also favorably received by the local press.

Kennedy's Legacy

By the end of 1961, 500 Peace Corps volunteers had been trained and were on duty in 9 countries. Several hundred more were training for posts in other countries. In addition to teaching in Ghana, Nigeria, and the Philippines, volunteers were involved in community work in St. Lucia, rural public works in Pakistan, and road surveying in Tanzania. The new agency had put the Peace Corps into action on three continents in less than a year.

By the end of 1962, Peace Corps programs had spread to 22 more countries in Africa, Asia, and South America—including Afghanistan, Bolivia, Iran, the Ivory Coast, Nepal, and Turkey—and the number of volunteers in the field had jumped to more than 2,800. A year later, the agency had 7,000 volunteers and trainees in 44 countries. Teaching was still the major occupation, with 55 percent of volunteers working in education. In the next largest category, 25.6 percent of volunteers were involved in community development—working with citizens' groups to improve their local environments. The remaining 20 percent worked on projects in agriculture, health care, and public works.

During the early 1960s, the Peace Corps was considered one of the brightest stars of the New Frontier, the term Kennedy coined for his administration. The strong identification of the agency with the youthful and idolized president nurtured the Peace Corps's growth and popularity; it was also felt by the young volunteers, many of whom had been inspired to join the corps by Kennedy himself. The president, in turn, demonstrated his enthusiasm for the program by visiting volunteers in Latin America, talking with staffers in Washington, and, whenever possible, meeting with groups of new trainees before they left for assignment.

The special relationship between Kennedy and the Peace Corps was noticed even in foreign countries. In the Dominican Republic, the volunteers were affectionately known as *hijos de Kennedy*—Kennedy's children. Local peoples

Peace Corps education volunteer Carol Waymire gets a boost from one of her Ghanaian students in 1961. By the end of the next year, the infant agency had more than 2,800 volunteers working on projects in 31 developing nations around the world.

in Africa came to call volunteers *wakina Kennedy*, or followers of Kennedy, making it seem as if the young men and women were the president's special ambassadors.

Set against this background, the assassination of the president in Dallas, Texas, on November 22, 1963, was a particularly devastating blow to Peace Corps volunteers around the world. Nevertheless, they continued their assignments, dedicating their efforts to his memory. One young female volunteer wrote, "I am proud to have been a part of an already-established living memorial to Kennedy: the Peace Corps."

Growth Under President Johnson

The Peace Corps staff and volunteers were reassured by support from Lyndon B. Johnson, who became president after Kennedy's death. Under the Johnson administration the corps continued its growth, with volunteer strength reaching 10,000 in 1964 and more than 15,000 in 1966.

Peace Corps volunteers welcome President Lyndon B. Johnson to Honduras in 1968. Johnson was able to inspire perseverance in the corps's young workers after John F. Kennedy's tragic death in 1963.

The agency grew in fiscal size as well. After its initial congressional appropriation of $30 million in September 1961, the Peace Corps, like any other federal bureau, relied on Congress for its annual budget. The federal funds allotted for the Peace Corps grew along with the number of volunteers, from $59 million in 1963 to $95.5 million in 1964 and $104.1 million in 1965. Shriver took care to point out to Congress that the cost per volunteer (the yearly amount to keep one volunteer overseas—including transportation, training, a $75-per-month allowance, and Washington staff costs) decreased as the volunteer ranks grew: $9,074 per volunteer in 1963, but only $7,809 per volunteer by 1965.

Shriver was able to keep these costs down by controlling the growth of staff in Washington. Between 1963 and 1966, while the overseas component of the Peace Corps was rapidly expanding, the staff at headquarters stayed at 650. The Peace Corps reached a peak in 1966; that year, it had the largest number of volunteers—15,556—and, until the 1980s, the biggest budget—$114 million. In that same year, the agency underwent another major change when Sargent Shriver resigned.

President Johnson had put Shriver in charge of his War on Poverty, based in the Office of Economic Opportunity. For months Shriver continued to head both the poverty program and the Peace Corps, spending half-days at each agency. Gradually, he spent less and less time at the Peace Corps, until his attendance there was down to one day a week. Although Shriver was reluctant to leave the agency, Johnson insisted that his full-time efforts were needed on the antipoverty program.

The president named Jack Hood Vaughn as the second director of the Peace Corps. Vaughn had a long history of service in U.S. foreign-aid agencies. Beginning in 1949, he served with the U.S. Information Agency in Latin America. He was later transferred to the International Cooperation Administration, serving in Latin America and West Africa. Shriver had initially brought Vaughn into the agency in 1961 as director of all Latin American Peace Corps programs. Then, in the spring of 1964, Johnson chose Vaughn to be his ambassador to Panama. Less than a year later, the president named him assistant secretary of state for inter-American affairs, a leading foreign-service post for Latin American policy. Finally, in 1966, Vaughn returned to the Peace Corps as its director.

Vaughn was as enthusiastic about the corps as his predecessor had been. One difference between the two directors, however, was in management style: Vaughn had a calm, low-key manner, as opposed to the energy and turbulence that seemed to characterize Shriver's administration. But the directors also had their similarities. Like Shriver, Vaughn believed in an extensive program, saying at one press conference that he looked forward to a time when Peace Corps volunteers would be stationed in every village in Africa, Asia, and Latin America. During the first year of Vaughn's term, the program spread to many new countries, including Botswana, Chad, Mauritania, South Korea, Micronesia, Guyana, and Libya.

Vaughn spent much of his first year traveling around the world to meet with his overseas staff and inviting returned volunteers into his office to discuss the agency's strengths and weaknesses. After a year, he was ready to make some changes in agency policy. One of his key changes was to stress quality over quantity: He decided to cut back on the number of volunteers to ensure that a good job existed for every volunteer in the field and that every volunteer was well prepared for his or her field assignment.

One of the Peace Corps's persistent problems had been the gap between the need of Third World countries for skilled help and the type of volunteer applying to join the agency—usually a college graduate with a general background in the liberal arts. Whereas these young Americans were knowledgeable in such subjects as literature, the arts, and the social sciences, they lacked specific skills in mathematical, scientific, and technical areas. Third World countries, however, were primarily interested in volunteers with training in the latter—particularly in agriculture, health care, forestry, and engineering.

Sometimes the deficiencies of the volunteers could be overcome by special-skill training. In Chile, many young "generalist" volunteers were trained to contribute to the country's reforestation project. They successfully worked with villagers in planting and caring for more than 5 million new trees on the barren slopes of the Andes.

In the African nation of Malawi, generalists were successfully trained to give tuberculosis skin tests and to read the results. Even though they had no medical background, the volunteers were taught how to recognize the symptoms of this life-threatening disease—such as coughing, chest pain, night sweats, and loss of weight—and to help control it by administering medicine and monitoring the progress of the patients.

Though these two programs were successful in using generalists trained in specific skills, many other projects in community development and public health had failed. Volunteers were sometimes sent into localities with vague assignments and left to flounder, lacking clear direction. Brent Ashabranner, who was now a deputy director of the agency, wrote about Vaughn's new philosophy: "The message that began to be heard and understood was that numbers were no longer the important thing. What was important were clearly defined projects with clearly defined volunteer responsibilities for which persons with liberal arts backgrounds could be clearly trained."

In addition to this change in program philosophy, the Peace Corps under Vaughn strengthened the training program it provided for its recruits. Many volunteers complained that the training, much of which was conducted by college teachers at schools and universities across the country, was too academic and did not give them sufficient technical and language skills. Vaughn now increased significantly the amount of time spent on language instruction, relocated most of the training programs to the countries of assignment, and made sure that instructors knew each volunteer's specific project.

In 1968, Vaughn decided that a still smaller Peace Corps would increase efficiency. Even at that time some programs—particularly in India, Micronesia, the Philippines, and Colombia—had too many volunteers for too few jobs. Many of the foreign governments agreed with this move. India clearly stated

A Nepali language instructor works with Peace Corps trainees at the University of California at Davis in 1968. Improvements in the agency's training program under Director Jack Hood Vaughn—including an increased amount of time spent on language instruction—led to a more efficient corps.

that it wanted fewer volunteers with more sophisticated skills. The Philippine government told the corps that it preferred to have a small number of education volunteers with classroom experience rather than a large number of unskilled generalists.

The Turbulent War Years

While Peace Corps administrators worked hard to perfect the internal workings of the agency, world events sometimes affected operations in ways that could not be avoided. After 1966, U.S. involvement in the Vietnam War cast a dark shadow over the positive work the Peace Corps was doing throughout the world.

Vietnam, a former French colony, had been partitioned into a western-oriented government in the south and a communist government in the north. When North Vietnam sought to reunite the country under a communist regime, the United States intervened to bolster the South Vietnamese government. U.S. military involvement in the conflict grew throughout the 1960s.

College students across the country angrily criticized President Johnson for continuing to send U.S. troops to fight in Vietnam. Many of them accused the Peace Corps of hypocrisy in light of the fierce war the government was perpetuating in Southeast Asia. Antiwar activists spoke out against joining the Peace Corps, charging that its ideals had been betrayed by the government's involvement in the Vietnam War. Many volunteers spoke out against the war and became involved in antiwar demonstrations overseas. Indeed, some of the male volunteers had joined the corps because it delayed their military service for two years.

Even though there was pressure from the White House, the State Department, and some congressmen to curb volunteer protest, only one young man

Antiwar protesters in a 1969 march on the Capitol hold aloft a Vietcong flag (left, representing the guerrilla group fighting U.S. forces in Vietnam) and an American flag with hearts in place of stars. In the late 1960s, opposition to U.S. involvement in the Vietnam War caused a marked decrease in applications for Peace Corps service.

was dismissed from the corps because of his stand on the Vietnam War. This case, however, created a furor in the press and only increased the anti–Peace Corps sentiment on college campuses. Peace Corps volunteers posted in Chile put together a petition in May 1967 that called for the cessation of American bombing of North Vietnam and the start of negotiations to end the war. The American ambassador to Chile warned the volunteers that if their names appeared in the Chilean newspapers, they would be expelled from the country. Vaughn was also adamantly opposed to the publication of the petition and threatened the volunteers with dismissal from the corps.

Volunteer Bruce Murray, a music teacher stationed in Chile, wrote to Vaughn to protest the director's strictures against volunteers speaking out on U.S. foreign policy. He sent copies of his letter to the press. After the letter was published in a Chilean newspaper he was expelled from the Peace Corps. Upon returning home, Murray learned that he no longer had a military deferment and would soon be drafted. The government also refused to give him an occupational deferment from the military to continue his teaching career.

A court case ensued, and the judge found in favor of Murray, supporting his right to free speech. The judge also reinstated Murray's military deferment. The Murray case caused much discussion and agonizing reappraisal within the corps as Vaughn and his staff wrestled with the problem of volunteer discontent. The staff worried that antiwar protests would cause them to lose the support of the American people and members of Congress. But the agency also realized that any strong crackdown or wholesale termination of volunteers would hurt the image of the Peace Corps on college campuses. As the war continued into 1968, all agency restrictions on volunteer antiwar activities were relaxed. The Peace Corps found it had to rely on the volunteers' common sense to keep their protests reasonable and under control.

Some of the college discontent with the Peace Corps can be noted in the shrinking number of applications to the agency during the war years. From a high of 42,000 in 1966, the number of applicants decreased to 35,000 in 1967, then 30,000 the next year, 24,000 in 1969, and bottomed out at 19,000 in 1970.

As the 1960s ended, the Peace Corps had matured. Better training, well-defined job assignments, and more skilled volunteers characterized agency operations in 55 Third World countries. "I would have to say that volunteers today are more knowledgeable, more inquisitive, more activist than when I first came to the Peace Corps, but they are not necessarily happier," said Jack Vaughn in 1969. Volunteers now had a more realistic view of the enormity of the task the Peace Corps had undertaken.

*Volunteer Dick Kirby advises a Venezuelan man on home construction in
1969. Kirby, who holds a bachelor's degree in industrial design, represented
the Peace Corps's new emphasis on specialized volunteers in the late 1960s
and early 1970s.*

FOUR

Growing Pains

With the election of Richard M. Nixon to the presidency in 1968, the Peace Corps went through a period of deep uncertainty. Many remembered the negative remarks Eisenhower's vice-president had made about the Peace Corps in his 1960 campaign against John F. Kennedy. There were even rumors circulating around Washington that President Nixon would discontinue the program.

Although these rumors proved untrue, Nixon did name a new director of the Peace Corps, 34-year-old Joseph H. Blatchford. He was relatively unknown in Peace Corps circles but had solid experience in developing South American aid programs. In the early 1960s, he had organized a privately funded organization, called ACCION, to undertake community development projects in Latin America. In its first 8 years, ACCION sent more than 1,000 Americans to Latin America to work in civic development, job training, construction, and education projects. During that time, Blatchford was successful in soliciting money and services worth approximately $9 million from 3,000 different companies.

Despite Blatchford's impressive qualifications, the Peace Corps had difficulty adjusting to the change from two supportive Democratic administrations under presidents Kennedy and Johnson to a wary Republican one under Nixon. There was tension and hostility among staffers toward the new director. Regardless of internal dissension, however, Blatchford had clear ideas on the direction in

59

President Richard M. Nixon congratulates Winifred Blatchford on the ap-pointment of her husband, Joseph (center), to Peace Corps director in May 1969. Blatchford pledged to lead the corps in a new, more efficient direction.

which he wanted to lead the Peace Corps. "We promise no panacea and the times have robbed us of the euphoric thrill found in leadership of a youth movement," Blatchford wrote in 1970 in *Foreign Affairs*, a political-science journal. "But in the seventies, the Peace Corps can be more lean, more innovative, more capable—a contributor to substantial change in a decade which sorely needs it."

Blatchford's idea of a leaner and more capable corps was embodied in the set of "new directions" he established for the agency. One of his goals was aimed at the Peace Corps's overseas operations. Blatchford wanted the corps to work more closely with Third World nations in planning and selecting projects to meet their individual needs. The agency accomplished this goal by hiring more foreign staff to administer overseas projects. By 1973, 57 percent of the overseas administrative staff of the Peace Corps was composed of foreign nationals.

Two of Blatchford's new directions called for recruiting more skilled workers and enlisting 200 volunteer families to serve in the corps. As early as 1965,

Shriver had toyed with the idea of Peace Corps family service, but he had found the prospect costly and difficult. Blatchford had no greater success. And though both Shriver and Vaughn had recognized the need for skilled workers, they both had realized that the generalist college graduate was still the mainstay of the agency. Blatchford's drive for skilled recruits did meet with some success, however. The number of generalists in the Peace Corps dropped from 47 percent of volunteers in 1969 to 34 percent 3 years later. During the same period, the number of agricultural specialists increased from 6 to 11 percent; skilled workers from 1 to 5 percent; and volunteers with professional skills—such as doctors—from 14 to 21 percent.

Not only were the new recruits more skilled, they were also older. Under Blatchford's new policy, the average volunteer age rose from 23.9 to 27.1 years, with about 5 percent of volunteers over 50 years old. By recruiting older Americans—who were less likely to be antiwar protesters—Blatchford also

Volunteer Suzanne Michael works alongside members of a Nicaraguan cooperative to twine sisal that will be sewn into carpets with native, pre-Columbian designs. In the 1970s, Peace Corps director Blatchford called for closer cooperation with host countries to plan projects to meet their diverse individual needs.

sought to put an end to anti–Vietnam War protests by volunteers. He reestablished the policy of no tolerance for antiwar demonstrations and terminated 12 volunteers when they did not comply with the rule.

One highly publicized protest occurred in February 1970 at the American embassy in Tunisia during a visit by Secretary of State William Rogers. As Rogers spoke at a tea, antiwar Peace Corps volunteers wearing black armbands pointedly turned their faces to the wall. In another protest that angered Blatchford and the Nixon administration, 16 returned volunteers took over offices at the Peace Corps headquarters and unfurled a flag representing the Vietcong, the guerrilla group fighting U.S. forces in Vietnam. They flew the flag in full view of the White House for several hours before leaving peacefully.

The Peace Corps was no longer the darling of the presidency, and White House receptions for embarking volunteers seemed to be part of history. In addition to the administration's choice of an older, more conservative recruit as a more suitable representative for the voluntary organization, Blatchford toned down criticism at the agency's headquarters by using the five-year rule to weed out unsympathetic staffers. In 1971 he accepted the resignations of 93 senior

Indonesian youths call for the removal of Peace Corps volunteers in 1965. By forging closer ties to Communist China, Indonesia joined many other countries whose changing political climates caused the corps's withdrawal in the 1960s and early 1970s.

and experienced administrators, about 10 percent of the administrative staff, and 27 of the 55 overseas program directors.

Besides quelling the turmoil within his agency, Blatchford had to fight congressional attempts to cut the Peace Corps's $82 million budget for 1972. Angered by volunteers' antiwar demonstrations, Democratic congressman Otto Passman of Louisiana, chairman of the House Appropriations Subcommittee dealing with foreign aid, slashed the agency's budget by $10 million. Blatchford complained to the administration that he would have to call back 2,300 of the 8,000 volunteers if these cuts were allowed to stand. The budget crisis was partially alleviated when President Nixon gave the agency an extra $2.6 million and Blatchford effected savings of an additional $1.3 million. In the end no Peace Corps programs were cut, but the budget crunch only emphasized the agency's shaky foundation.

In the late 1960s and early 1970s, political change in the host countries affected Peace Corps operations overseas. Because of military coups and various other political crises, the corps was forced to leave nine different countries—Somalia, Libya, Guinea, Mauritania, Tanzania, Barbados, St. Lucia, Pakistan, and Thailand. (In later years, the corps was able to return to most of these countries.)

Reorganization and Turmoil

In July 1971 the Nixon administration made a major change in the Peace Corps's status. Nixon took away the agency's semiautonomous status by combining it with several other federal volunteer programs to form an independent federal umbrella agency called ACTION. The other units in ACTION were Volunteers in Service to America (VISTA), a group started by Johnson in 1964 and known as the "domestic Peace Corps" because of its work in locally sponsored projects in the United States; the Foster Grandparent Program (FGP), a unit comprised of low-income persons over 60 who provide companionship to mentally, physically, and emotionally handicapped children in institutions; and the Retired Senior Volunteer Program (RSVP), a group of older Americans who use their talents and expertise in community service. Other units in the new agency were the Service Corps of Retired Executives (SCORE), a volunteer organization of retired businessmen and -women who give advice to entrepreneurs on small-business problems; and the Active Corps of Executives (ACE), a supplement to SCORE whose members provide counseling on specialized business concerns.

Critics saw the reorganization as an attack on the Peace Corps's special identity and esprit de corps, a way to remove it from the public eye and diminish its favorable image among Americans. Supporters of the new agency said that the reorganization would increase the corps's efficiency as a bureaucracy, especially in handling its financial affairs. Blatchford was named head of ACTION; the Peace Corps director, now officially titled ACTION associate director for international operations, became subordinate to him.

The troubled Peace Corps had four different directors between 1971 and 1976. In 1973, cuts in staff and volunteer support services by ACTION director Michael Balzano, a former staff assistant at the Nixon White House, only worsened the political climate.

The turmoil within the agency mirrored the disturbances engulfing the Nixon administration, culminating in the president's resignation in August 1974 in the wake of the Watergate scandal. President Nixon was accused of authorizing a cover-up of a Republican party–sponsored break-in at the Democratic party headquarters in the Watergate office building in Washington, D.C. When Congress threatened to impeach Nixon, he resigned, and Vice-president Gerald Ford took over the presidency.

A Revitalized Corps

After Ford became chief executive, a feeling of stability descended upon the administration. Again the Peace Corps enjoyed strong presidential support. In March 1975, Ford appointed John Dellenback, a former Republican congressman from Oregon, director of the battered agency.

In this post-Vietnam era, Dellenback pledged to bring the Peace Corps back to life. With less than two years before the administration was voted out of office, Dellenback's promise could not be entirely fulfilled, but under his leadership the agency made many positive steps forward. One step was the formation of the Peace Corps's Information Collection and Exchange (ICE) program in 1975. ICE was the agency's first major attempt to collect and translate volunteers' knowledge and experience into manuals on subjects ranging from inland fisheries and grain storage to forest conservation and well construction. This information could be shared with development workers around the world.

Dellenback's staff was heartened by a revitalization of interest in the Peace Corps, as demonstrated by the dramatic increase in applicants—from 19,000 in 1970 to more than 30,000 in 1975. On the downside, the number of volunteers and trainees in the field had shrunk drastically, from 12,131 in 1969 to 5,958 in 1976, and the budget had decreased from $102 million to $81 million during that same period. Still, volunteers were serving in 68 countries, and there were more requests from developing nations than the agency could fill. Some Peace Corps advocates contend that training and programming actually improved during the turbulent period from 1969 to 1976.

The Carter Years: 1977–81

After the election of Democrat Jimmy Carter in 1976, many onlookers expected the Peace Corps to regain the attention and prized status that it had enjoyed during the Democratic Kennedy-Johnson years. One upbeat note was

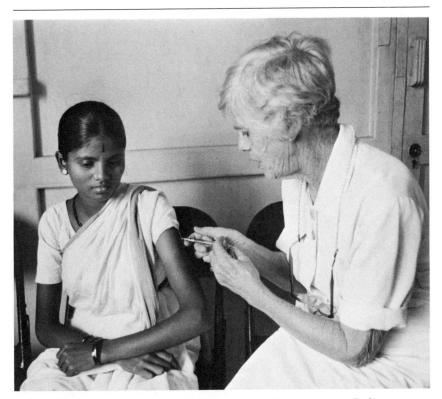

Peace Corps nurse Lillian Carter gives an injection to a young Indian woman in 1968. The mother of President Jimmy Carter served as a Peace Corps volunteer in India from 1966 to 1968.

that the new president's mother had been a Peace Corps volunteer: "Miz Lillian," as she was affectionately known, had served as a nurse in India from 1966 to 1968.

Carter appointed Samuel W. Brown, Jr., director of ACTION. Brown, a liberal activist, had served as the national volunteer coordinator for Democratic senator Eugene McCarthy's 1968 presidential campaign. He had also led an anti–Vietnam War march in Washington the following year. Brown's previous government service had been as state treasurer of Colorado.

After a six-month search, Brown appointed Carolyn R. Payton, a psychologist and former director of counseling at Howard University, to head the Peace Corps. The first black and the first woman to hold this position, Payton was not a newcomer to the agency. She had been a Peace Corps country director in the eastern Caribbean from 1966 to 1969.

Payton took over the agency at a time when it was described in a December 1977 *New York Times* article as "virtually invisible, a pale bureaucratic shadow of one of the most original ideas to come out of the turbulent 1960s." Her aim,

The first black American and the first woman to serve as Peace Corps director, Carolyn Payton was appointed at a low point in agency morale. Despite her ambitious plans for the corps, Payton resigned one year later after a conflict with AC-TION director Samuel W. Brown, Jr.

she said, was to boost morale among the headquarters staff, increase the number of volunteers, and attract more minorities to the agency. Although the agency had tried previously to increase minority participation at all levels within the corps, the results had always been disappointing. Payton believed that the appointment of a minority Peace Corps director would awaken the black community's interest in the Peace Corps.

In addition to the change in leadership, the corps's underlying philosophy was in a state of flux. The agency had had to adapt its policies and programs to changing conditions in the developing countries. The rise of nationalism in Third World states led them to prefer self-help programs over western voluntary groups such as the Peace Corps. Additionally, the countries with the most volunteers and the most cooperative governments were often the nations that were the least democratic; three of these countries—Chile, Korea, and the Philippines—had been criticized by President Carter for their human-rights violations. For the corps to survive in this critical environment, it was more important than ever for its volunteers to be well trained and for their projects to be worthwhile.

Finally, it was necessary to come to grips with the hard reality that the time for the sweeping idealism of the 1960s was over. The Peace Corps was not going to change the world. Was the Peace Corps making any headway in fostering development in Third World nations? The results were mixed. One former volunteer returned to India 10 years later to see that the poultry project he had helped initiate had grown enormously in the interim. But for every positive result there seemed to be a negative one, such as a former volunteer who told of an irrigation system he had built in a small village in Senegal that four years later was broken down and completely inoperative. Even his vegetable garden had been abandoned.

Before these philosophical questions could be addressed, a power struggle developed between Brown and Payton. The two disagreed violently on many issues, including individual project proposals, the number of countries the corps would serve, and the criteria the agency used to decide which areas to serve. Payton claimed that Brown had promised her at the time of her appointment that the Peace Corps would remain in all 62 countries it then served. The following year, however, Brown prepared a list of 14 nations to withdraw from, including Brazil, South Korea, Chile, Malaysia, Costa Rica, Jamaica, Tonga, Fiji, and Barbados. In addition, Payton claimed that under Brown's new Physical Quality of Life Index (PQLI), which determined whether to stay in or leave a country, the corps would be pulling out of almost all its Latin American and Asian programs and would send the bulk of its volunteers to Africa. Brown countered that some countries had undergone such extensive development that they no longer needed the corps, while others, such as Bangladesh, had no volunteers and needed them more.

It was, by all accounts, a nasty bureaucratic battle that came to a head at a regional Peace Corps conference in Morocco in November 1978. Friends and co-workers of the embattled Peace Corps director charged that Brown and his associates were ignoring Payton, trying to embarrass her and force her resignation. One night Brown called Payton's hotel room at midnight while she was meeting with her staff and told her in no uncertain terms to "get out of here." Brown insisted that he was in charge of making policy and claimed that Payton had consistently tried to undermine his authority. When President Carter sided with Brown, Payton left the corps. Her chief deputy quit in protest, and a number of other top staffers either were fired or quit. Payton labeled the event a purge.

Carter appointed a new director to fill the position vacated by Payton. He promised 42-year-old Richard Celeste a greater degree of autonomy for the corps. In May 1979, with Congress pressing for changes in the status of the corps—even going so far as to suggest that it be removed from ACTION altogether—Carter signed an executive order granting the Peace Corps special independence within the umbrella agency. He transferred the authority for running the agency from the director of ACTION back to the Peace Corps director. Celeste was thus given control of the agency's budget, policy, and personnel.

The Peace Corps at Twenty

Celeste used the upcoming 20th anniversary of John F. Kennedy's 2:00 A.M. campaign address at the University of Michigan—in which the presidential candidate had first mentioned a Peace Corps–type voluntary agency—as the kickoff for a major recruitment drive. Many Americans still expressed an interest in serving in the Peace Corps, but Celeste wanted to attract people who were more experienced in a wide variety of fields, from agriculture and auto mechanics to math and science.

Two decades before, developing nations were crying out for primary and secondary school teachers. A generation later, many of these same nations were graduating enough teachers to fill much of that need. Of the 40 percent of volunteers who were teaching in 1980, about one-half were involved in specialized programs such as literacy or vocational education.

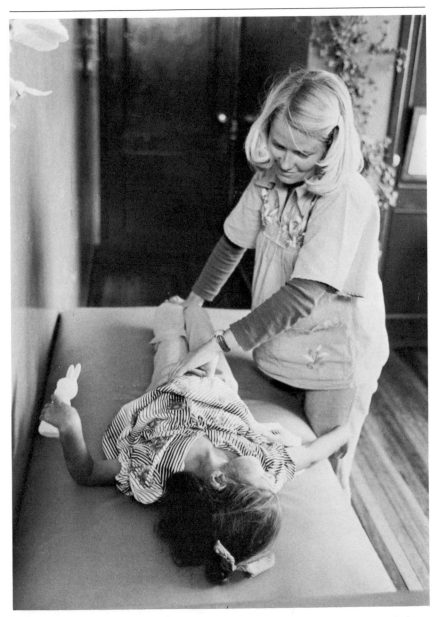

Toni Thomson, an occupational therapist, works with a mentally retarded girl at a psychiatric hospital in Conocoto, Ecuador, in 1977. Carolyn Payton charged that Latin American Peace Corps projects such as this one were endangered by ACTION director Brown's new criteria for needy countries.

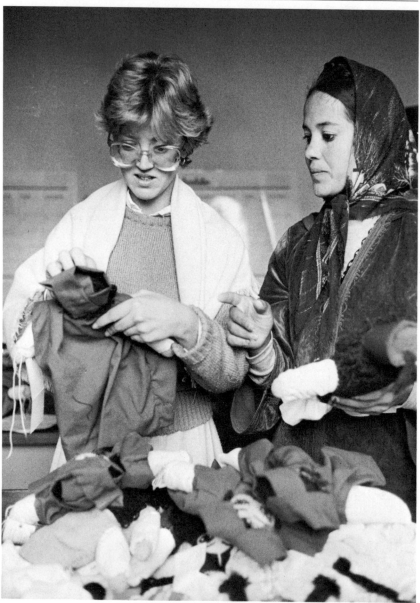

Peace Corps volunteer Phyllis Erikson inspects a handmade doll in a workshop in Temara, Morocco. Erikson's project, inspired by the corps's new emphasis on the role of women in development, involved helping a group of Moroccan women make and market the dolls.

Celeste's perceptions seemed to bear out the theories of the Nixon era, when the Peace Corps had first stressed the need to recruit skilled workers. Yet Celeste was aware of the limitations of this bias, noting that the Peace Corps could not be a job-placement agency. He also agreed with Brown's philosophy that when goals had been met, it was appropriate for the corps to withdraw from a country. He noted that because Bahrain, a small oil-rich nation in the Persian Gulf, had reached a point where it had the resources to fulfill its own development needs, the Peace Corps should withdraw. He also believed that the program in South Korea should be phased out.

Political instability again became a problem in some countries in the beginning of the 1980s, and Celeste had to remove volunteers from Afghanistan, Chad, Nicaragua, and El Salvador. In an increasingly tense, nationalistic world, security became a problem for Peace Corps volunteers. Since the agency's creation, only two volunteers had been taken hostage by antigovernment forces in their host countries. Botanist Dick Starr was kidnapped in February 1977 and held for three years by Colombian guerrillas; he was finally released after syndicated columnist Jack Anderson raised a $250,000 ransom for him. Volunteer Debbie Loff was held for 11 days in El Salvador in 1979 before she was released. Now, with an increasingly hostile atmosphere present in many Third World countries, Peace Corps administrators feared that more such incidents might occur.

Another concern had come to light in a 1978 study that showed that the bulk of volunteers were not working in the poorest and least-developed countries. This study also noted that in four of the world's poorest countries—India, Pakistan, Bangladesh, and Indonesia—the corps had no programs at all. Because of this realization, agency leaders decided to concentrate the volunteers' energy on meeting the basic human needs of what they termed the "absolute poor" in the developing world. In 1978 they incorporated a statement outlining this philosophy into the original Peace Corps Act. To put this mandate into action, administrators cut traditional English-teaching programs by an estimated 33 percent and gave higher priority to projects in the fields of health care, nutrition, food supply, and water.

Along with meeting basic human needs, the corps placed new emphasis on the role of women in development. In developing countries, women handle much of the farm labor, trade, and commerce in addition to performing domestic duties. A second amendment to the Peace Corps Act recognized this crucial role by redirecting energy toward projects to train rural women in skills in the areas of health care, nutrition, food production, and small-business development.

As the agency neared its 20th anniversary, volunteers registered increased satisfaction with their training and assignments. A survey in 1979 showed that 89 percent of volunteers felt satisfied that their job skills were well matched to their work assignments and 72 percent said that their field work had been clearly defined.

In the first 10 years of the Peace Corps, the young college graduate without any special training—the generalist—was the mainstay of the agency. In the second 10 years, emphasis had been placed on recruiting specialists—skilled workers and technicians, from carpenters to engineers. But as the number of applications began to drop significantly (only 13,661 in 1978, the lowest number since 1961) and the difficulty in recruiting specialists persisted, the Peace Corps again turned to generalists to meet its need for volunteers.

The agency realized that if generalist recruits were properly selected and trained in special skills they could make a valuable contribution. Its new recruiting slogan—The toughest job you'll ever love—reflected the corps's desire to again attract young college graduates. With this new emphasis on recruitment, applications rose in 1979 to 18,159, attesting to the success of the program. As the Carter presidency drew to a close, the agency had about 6,000 volunteers and trainees working in 62 countries.

The Peace Corps Under Loret Ruppe

Peace Corps supporters worried that Republican president Ronald Reagan, elected in 1980, would drastically cut or even eliminate the Peace Corps in his drive to cut the federal bureaucracy. Reagan's conservative supporters had never forgiven the agency for its outspoken criticism during the Vietnam War and for its beginnings as the brainchild of liberal Democrat John F. Kennedy. On the other hand, Reagan himself had emphasized volunteer service and more personal, one-on-one programs to meet social needs. The fate of the corps, still a part of the umbrella agency ACTION, lay in the hands of a new director.

Reagan appointed as director of the Peace Corps 45-year-old Loret Miller Ruppe, the co-chair of the 1980 Reagan-Bush campaign in Michigan. Although Ruppe had an impressive background working in civic voluntary organizations, she had no experience in overseas work and no other Peace Corps–type qualifications. This was to be her first salaried position. Many staffers and former Peace Corps volunteers worried that she would fail to hold the agency together. But Ruppe had a specific agenda for the Peace Corps and a host of unexpected talents. Harris Wofford, one of Sargent Shriver's original staff,

Peace Corps director Loret Ruppe on a tour of Ghana in the mid-1980s. Under Ruppe's leadership the corps focused on practical projects, such as those that helped people earn money.

praised her strong administrative abilities and solid knowledge of how to maneuver politically to win congressional support for the corps.

Reagan's appointee to head ACTION caused alarm, however—especially in Congress. The nomination of Thomas Pauken, who had worked in military intelligence in Vietnam, was controversial because the Peace Corps had always taken great pains to dissociate itself from spying. Any connection with espionage, no matter how innocent, could endanger programs in many countries. To solve this dilemma, a political compromise was worked out in December 1981: Pauken's nomination was confirmed but the Peace Corps once again became an independent agency, completely separate from ACTION.

Under Ruppe's full control, the Peace Corps became "Reaganized"—slightly less idealistic, with more of an emphasis on pragmatic projects such as those that promote small-business development. In the fall of 1982, Ruppe launched a new program, called Competitive Enterprise Development, to promote business-oriented projects that would foster economic prosperity in Third World nations. Most of the developing countries were interested in projects that enabled their citizens to earn money. To do this, they needed to learn business skills such as bookkeeping, marketing, and sales techniques. The

73

business enterprises helped by the Peace Corps ran the gamut from helping African beekeepers market their honey to working with the Turkish Tourism Bureau to teach hotel and restaurant owners accounting principles.

In addition to the new emphasis on small-business development, Ruppe launched several new programs in the Caribbean, Central America, and Africa. The Caribbean Basin Initiative, the Initiative for Central America, and the Africa Food Systems Initiative help inhabitants in those areas solve development problems particular to each region.

The director also made a significant policy change when she formalized cooperation with other development agencies within and outside of the U.S. government. In the early days of the Peace Corps, Sargent Shriver had

President Ronald Reagan gives Africa-bound volunteers an official send-off in 1985. The Peace Corps's Africa Food Systems Initiative, launched that year, was a concerted effort by the corps, AID, and the World Bank to combat the effects of drought on Africa's food supply.

A policeman drives a starving crowd away from food supplies in a village in the Sudan in 1985. The Peace Corps launched a program in the Sudan in 1984 but was soon forced to cancel it when the Sudanese government forged closer ties to Libya, a country hostile to the United States.

shunned ties with traditional foreign-aid units, such as AID. He wanted to keep the corps independent of agencies that had been branded culturally insensitive. But since those early days both agencies had changed, and if the Peace Corps no longer had a holier-than-thou attitude, AID had more respect for the work of the corps. Besides, by 1985 former volunteers made up 13.5 percent of AID staff, and in 1981 Peter McPherson, a former Peace Corps volunteer, was appointed to head the agency. Within a short time, AID and the Peace Corps were working together on more than 100 projects in 30 different countries. In 1983 the two agencies launched a small-project assistance program whereby AID would fund small, self-help Peace Corps projects in 40 countries.

This close working relationship with AID gave the corps the financial support it needed at a time when budget problems threatened the agency's operations.

Loret Ruppe and Sargent Shriver lead a march to John F. Kennedy's grave site at Arlington National Cemetery in 1986. The mass march was a somber event in the otherwise festive yearlong celebration of the Peace Corps's 25th anniversary.

Although the agency had recently reversed its decline in funding, because of inflation the purchasing power of those dollars had shrunk. With this financial squeeze, the headquarters and support staff had decreased along with the number of volunteers. In 1982, volunteer ranks had sunk to 5,380, the lowest level since 1962.

With the budget crunch, certain overseas operations had to be curtailed. Ruppe directed a review of programs around the world and reluctantly decided to withdraw from Colombia, South Korea, and the Ivory Coast. These countries would be hurt the least if volunteers were withdrawn, she reasoned. Over the next few years, volunteers left Chile, Malaysia, Brazil, Grenada, Oman, and El Salvador for financial, political, and other reasons.

Another way the agency dealt with shrinking financial resources was to accept support from the host countries. Many nations contributed housing, office space, computers, and transportation to ease the corps's overseas expenses. But Ruppe was not about to let the agency wither away. She was determined that the Peace Corps rebuild from this low point. With her imaginative new programs and extensive political contacts, plus the goodwill felt toward the agency, Ruppe began to turn the funding problem around. By 1985 she had successfully fended off budget cuts and convinced Congress to set a goal of 10,000 volunteers by 1992.

When the Peace Corps marked its 25th anniversary in 1986, Ruppe was pleased to report that the agency was on a "forward roll." Funding for the corps had reached a high of $130 million, and the number of volunteers had risen to 6,264—its highest point since 1979.

In September 1986, nearly 7,000 former volunteers met in Washington, D.C., to cap off a year of anniversary activities. The celebration had begun in October 1985 at the University of Michigan with the first of nearly 30 official discussions and forums on the corps's history, its successes and failures, and ways in which the agency could do better. The Washington, D.C., celebration, held over the course of four days, was highlighted by a keynote speech by Philippine president Corazon Aquino and speeches by the agency's first director, Sargent Shriver, and its longest-serving director, Loret Miller Ruppe. There was also a mass march across the Potomac to the Kennedy grave site at Arlington National Cemetery.

Proposals for future Peace Corps activities that came out of the yearlong examination included encouraging the Peace Corps to reach larger countries such as China, India, Pakistan, and Brazil and to increase its cooperation with other development agencies; requesting Congress to fund the agency for more than one year at a time; varying the length of service for highly skilled volunteers; and expanding the corps's system for evaluating and monitoring projects.

Ruppe was pleased to describe in her April 1988 report to Congress how the Peace Corps was fulfilling these proposals. She announced that the agency had been asked back to Pakistan, which it had left in 1967, and was working with China to develop a program for that nation. She reported that the corps was in a "growth pattern" and by year's end would have 6,600 volunteers working in 67 countries around the world.

The future looked promising for the Peace Corps. Finally, it was firmly established within the federal government, within the Third World community, and within the hearts and minds of the American public. Although budget problems within the U.S. government threatened to delay Ruppe's goal of 10,000 volunteers for several years, the agency continued to work on realizing the three main goals expressed by President Kennedy in 1961: to provide skilled workers to developing countries, to make friends for America among these nations, and to promote American understanding of Third World nations.

Volunteer Janet Rich checks a woman's blood pressure at a mother-child health-care clinic in Torodi, Niger. Although the Peace Corps is run from its headquarters in Washington, D.C., the organization's heart is in the individual projects it sponsors around the world.

FIVE

Today's Peace Corps

Although the Peace Corps headquarters is located in Washington, D.C., the heart of the agency is spread out over the myriad projects run by individual volunteers. The entire organization is dedicated to fostering the work of these individuals in small towns and villages in developing countries around the world.

The headquarters houses the more than 500 members of the agency's administrative staff. The staff is divided into three major units: the first deals with recruitment and placement of volunteers; the second, with overseeing projects in the countries around the world and training recruits to meet the needs of specific projects; and the third, with managing the agency itself—from paying the bills to hiring headquarters personnel.

In addition to the agency's headquarters staff, it has approximately 180 agency workers at 16 recruitment offices in major cities across the country. Overseas, the corps employs approximately 180 Americans and 300 foreign nationals to supervise field projects in more than 60 host countries.

The director and deputy director oversee the entire Peace Corps operation, from the headquarters staff, the satellite offices, and the overseas offices down to the individual volunteer in the field. The Peace Corps's director reports to the president.

The largest percentage of volunteers work in education. In addition to teaching English to 12- to 18-year-old boys, Jeff McCaskey—shown here with students at the Sri Chulachuli Secondary School in Nepal—worked on a number of agricultural projects.

Field Projects

For the thousands of volunteers in the field, headquarters can be half a world away, and their attention is directed primarily toward the projects assigned to them. These projects cover a full range of developmental needs, including education, agriculture, health care and nutrition, fisheries, forestry, water and sanitation, and small-business development.

Education

The largest proportion of volunteers, approximately 29 percent, work in education. Although education projects have been among the Peace Corps's major successes, some development experts claim that because education is not a basic human need—as are food, water, shelter, and health care—it should not be given priority in programming. However, like her predecessors, Loret Ruppe decided that education was an important need and that developing countries need help with their education programs.

To fit their education projects to the developing nations' need for more practical training, the corps has de-emphasized the teaching of English in favor of vocational education, math and science teaching, teacher training, and special education for physically and mentally disabled students. The only classroom teachers are in remote areas where the host country has difficulty filling teaching posts with its own citizens.

This new focus in education is typified by Janet Lea Barnett, a graduate in mathematics from Colorado State University. As a volunteer, Barnett taught math at one of the largest high schools in Bambari, Central African Republic. She noted that because math is the basis for such advanced studies as engineering, it is of paramount importance for developing countries. Other knowledge crucial to the development of Third World nations includes chemistry, biology, physics, and general science.

Volunteer Peggy Braun, deaf herself, teaches mathematics to hearing-impaired students at the Southeast Asia Institute for the Deaf in the Philippines. Special-needs projects such as this one are among the most important contributions the Peace Corps makes in the field of education.

Practical education in skills ranks second to such academic subjects. In Western Samoa, volunteer Terry Kelly taught motor mechanics to young men so they could repair cars, motorcycles, and buses. The project was supported by an AID grant of $2,200 for tools to outfit a training shop. Kelly taught his Samoan class how to make their own car parts as well as to do repair work. He said his greatest satisfaction came from seeing students repair broken motors and then hearing the motors roar to life in the shop.

One of the most important contributions the Peace Corps makes in education is teaching special-needs students who are deaf, blind, or otherwise physically or mentally disabled. Before the agency became involved in special education, these children had remained uneducated. When volunteer Dennis Drake arrived on the island of Bohol in the Philippines, for example, there were no schools for deaf children there. He went from one remote mountain village to another to convince parents that their hearing-impaired children would benefit from an education. Within two years, 40 students were enrolled in the Jagna School for the Deaf and Blind that Drake had helped establish.

Agriculture

Agricultural projects occupy approximately 25 percent of all volunteers. More than one-fifth of the Third World—an estimated 600 million people—suffers from hunger or starvation. Therefore, increasing food production is a priority in the poorest of developing nations.

The agency tailors each project to suit the particular area and need. In past agricultural projects, volunteers have assisted islanders in the Caribbean in controlling insect infestations; helped Micronesian beekeepers to increase the profits of their honey harvest by improving bee colonies; and introduced farmers in Togo to plowing with oxen instead of using old, inefficient short-handled hoes. This last project was so successful that it tripled the amount of land area the farmers could use, and other development groups decided to copy the project throughout the country.

Health and Nutrition

Health and nutrition problems abound in the developing world. Experts estimate that 20 to 25 million children under the age of 5 die each year in the Third World. Most of these deaths are from common, curable diseases such as diarrhea and respiratory infections. To aid in the fight against disease in developing nations, the Peace Corps assigns approximately 12 percent of its volunteers to health projects.

Agriculture volunteer Scott Kirchoff (right) has an extensive background in plant and soil science. His dry-land farming experiment in the Tigre Province in Ethiopia will help determine the best method for farming in the arid region.

Because it is difficult to attract doctors, nurses, and other health-care professionals to the corps, the majority of volunteers in health projects are generalists trained to do specific tasks. Approximately 40 percent are nurses, nutritionists, and other professionals. The health volunteers work mainly with people at the highest risk for disease, such as pregnant and nursing mothers, infants, and young children.

Fisheries

The Peace Corps has started so many fish-farming projects around the world that agency staffers refer to the program as the "blue revolution" (as opposed to the "green" agricultural revolution in Third World nations, in which the amount of crops under cultivation has grown dramatically). In the 1960s the agency started off slowly, with only a handful of volunteers working in this field each year. However, these projects were so successful that by the late 1980s

Marine biologist Gene Feltman (center) works on fishery projects for Western Samoa's Ministry of Economic Development. The Peace Corps's aquaculture (fish-farming) projects have been extremely successful.

the corps annually assigned about eight percent of its volunteers to work in fisheries.

Aquaculture, or fish farming, is important to developing nations because common, inexpensive fish such as carp and tilapia are a good source of protein that people like to eat and that sell well. Peace Corps volunteers help villagers build, stock, and manage man-made fish ponds. The Peace Corps has found that an investment in fish farming from a man-made pond makes more money for a small farmer than an investment in popular livestock such as chickens, rabbits, or goats.

Volunteer Roger Palm set up a fish-farming project in Zaire. Palm first had to locate a group of farmers who were willing to make the commitment to start a fishery. He helped them choose sites for their ponds and taught them how to build dikes and canals. Once they finished building the ponds, Palm showed the farmers how to divert water from springs and rivers to fill them. Finally, Palm introduced the farmers to a new type of fish, the Nile tilapia, and stocked the ponds with the fish. The farmers fed and cared for the fish for six months and then harvested their "crop" by draining the ponds.

"I helped them market the fish," remembered Palm. "The people in my village and the next loved the fish so much that each harvest was eaten fresh . . . the program was a great success."

Forestry

Approximately eight percent of Peace Corps volunteers work in forestry and natural-resources programs. Environmental experts began to realize fully in the 1980s that the loss of forestland in the developing world had become a worldwide crisis. These forests ordinarily prevent flooding, soil erosion, air pollution, and damage to plant life. Another immediate effect of forest shrinkage in the Third World is the loss of wood fuel needed to heat homes and cook food.

Peace Corps forestry projects typically involve tree planting, especially in sub-Saharan Africa, where projects aim to hold back the desert. Other projects revolve around agroforestry, a new field that combines growing trees and food crops and animal farming. Forestry volunteers teach native farmers the benefits of growing trees as a source of fuel, as a salable crop, and as protection for soil from the wind and rain.

Water and Sanitation

With sub-Saharan Africa suffering from droughts that have devastated harvests and caused famine in several countries, water projects have taken on a new

Peace Corps volunteers work with villagers to repair a dam in Burkina Faso. Inhabitants of this region are dependent on dams to trap and conserve rain— their only source of water.

significance in the Peace Corps. In the 1980s, eight percent of the volunteers worked on water and sanitation projects, mainly in Africa.

Generally, these projects involve developing water resources for drinking and for use in farming. Volunteers help clean up polluted water supplies and aid in building sanitary latrines or toilets. Water and sanitation projects have reduced the incidence of malaria in Thailand, introduced sanitary toilets to many parts of the Philippines, and brought piped-in water to remote villages in Kenya.

In Burkina Faso, a small, landlocked country in West Africa, volunteer Steve Evett helped villagers build small earthen dams and dikes to collect rainwater— the villagers' only source of water for use in irrigation. The increased water supply allowed the villagers to increase their rice production and thus made a real difference in their lives. Evett said the project was frustrating at times, because violent rainstorms could easily destroy weak dams and dikes. But he concluded that such projects were essential, especially in African villages.

86

Small-Business Development

About five percent of Peace Corps volunteers work in developing small businesses in Third World countries. Their projects include helping villagers in Papua New Guinea start and manage a vegetable growers' cooperative and helping African women establish a small handicrafts industry.

Twenty-five-year-old volunteer Rita Jeanne Murphy worked with women in the Dominican Republic to help them sell purses and place mats they had woven from plantain- and banana-tree fibers. "I am very happy and proud of these women who, from their own initiative and hard work, created jobs for themselves and a better life for their families," said Murphy.

Host Countries

For administrative purposes, the Peace Corps divides the developing world into three main regions: North Africa, the Near East, Asia, and the Pacific Islands (NANEAP); Inter-America; and Africa.

NANEAP

The Peace Corps has grouped the 21 countries it serves in these 4 regions into 1 sector for organizational purposes. Because this is an artificial grouping—the countries differ in culture, geography, and development needs—the agency has no cohesive set of plans for these regions and must draw up specific plans for each division. The corps has more than 1,200 volunteers in this grouping, with the largest numbers in Thailand, the Philippines, and Morocco.

North Africa/Near East: These regions lack good farmland and have poor health conditions, both of which lead to a high mortality rate and a low life expectancy of about 55 years. (The United States has an average life expectancy of about 75.) The Peace Corps's aim for this area is to expand agriculture, increase rural health care and water resources, expand small-business opportunities, and improve basic education and practical job skills.

Special Peace Corps achievements in this region include a volunteer project in Morocco to teach parents of children with cerebral palsy how to work with their disabled youngsters to strengthen their bodies. Peace Corps volunteers also helped rural villagers in Yemen rebuild their homes after a major earthquake killed many people and destroyed thousands of homes in December 1982.

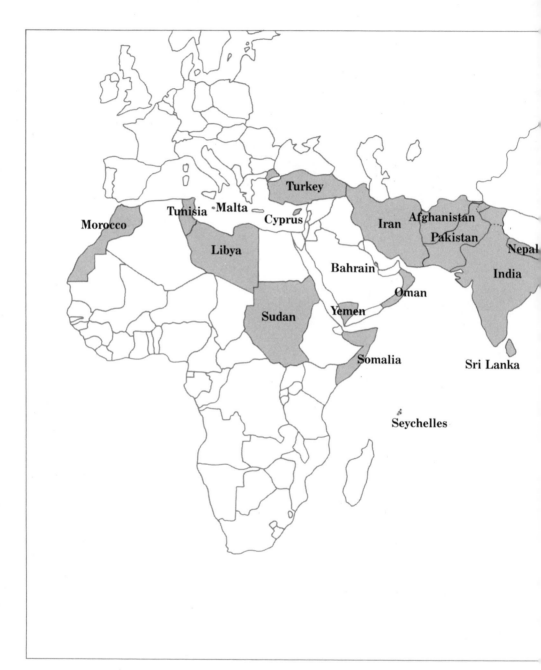

Shaded areas represent Peace Corps host countries in North Africa, the Near East, Asia, and the Pacific Islands (NANEAP) from 1961 to 1989.

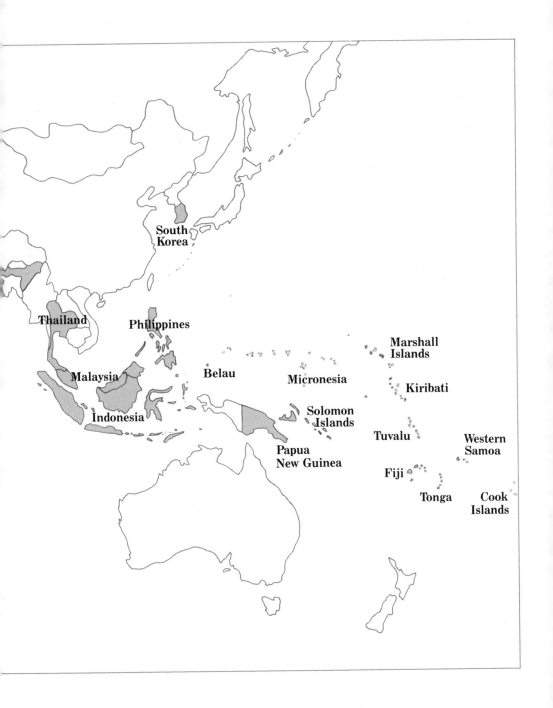

South
Korea

Thailand

Philippines

Malaysia

Belau

Marshall
Islands

Micronesia

Kiribati

Indonesia

Solomon
Islands

Tuvalu

Western
Samoa

Papua
New Guinea

Fiji

Tonga

Cook
Islands

Education volunteer Terry Lajtha (left) has her fortune told at a Moroccan market as her interpreter and fellow teacher looks on. English education—both at the high school level and in teacher-training programs—is a priority for Moroccan Peace Corps planners.

Asia: Besides assisting with basic human-needs projects, volunteers posted in Asian countries help plant trees in areas denuded of forests and work to expand small-business opportunities. In Thailand and the Philippines, two of the region's more developed countries, assistance is concentrated in rural areas.

Peace Corps achievements in the Asian region include a project in Nepal in which volunteers trained more than 750 teachers in math, science, and English. The Peace Corps workers also trained teachers in remote areas of the country, where an acute shortage of teachers existed. In an agency project in Sri Lanka, education volunteers worked with school staffs and more than 400 deaf students to improve special-education programs.

Pacific Islands: In this region of island countries, the Peace Corps faces the challenge of fostering development without threatening the environment. The corps must also overcome other regional problems, including a limited fresh water supply, limited farmland, poor roads and bridges, a small population (and thus a manpower shortage), and few natural resources.

Shaded areas represent Peace Corps presence in the Inter-American region, 1961–89.

One volunteer in the Solomon islands established an aluminum container recycling business that helped eliminate litter in the capital city. Several other volunteer civil engineers stationed on the second largest of the Seychelles islands helped build a major water treatment, storage, and distribution system.

Inter-America

Most poor inhabitants of the Caribbean islands and Central and South America live in rural areas with minimal educational and health facilities. The recent deterioration of the region's economies has left governments with even less money to spend on development. With little hope of receiving economic assistance from foreign countries, this region must rely on self-help projects to make money for its inhabitants. Since the Peace Corps's creation in 1961, more than 25,000 volunteers have worked in 28 nations in this region. In 1988 there were more than 1,500 volunteers working in 17 countries, with the largest contingents in Honduras, Guatemala, Ecuador, and Costa Rica.

The Peace Corps's Caribbean Basin Initiative aims to improve conditions in Central America and the Caribbean by developing small businesses, especially agricultural ones. Volunteers have set up a variety of small projects to generate income for villagers and have trained businessmen in accounting, management, and marketing skills to make their enterprises more profitable.

Pat Duffy goes over the books in a farmers' cooperative in Costa Rica, where she teaches business and accounting. Under the Initiative for Central America, volunteers help develop natural resources and expand small-business opportunities in Belize, Costa Rica, Guatemala, and Honduras.

92

Under the Initiative for Central America, volunteers help villagers in Belize, Costa Rica, Guatemala, and Honduras increase their production of food, goods, services, and natural resources. The corps also provides these countries with volunteers skilled as teachers and health and nutrition technicians. Special emphasis has been placed on training foreign nationals to teach blind, deaf, mentally retarded, and learning-disabled students.

Peace Corps volunteers in Guatemala are working with local authorities to manage the aggressive African insects known as killer bees. Also in Guatemala, volunteer nurses in a community-health project performed 14,000 examinations and trained nearly 300 native health-care workers. Volunteers in Costa Rica helped poor rural families build 270 homes. And Peace Corps workers in the Eastern Caribbean helped start businesses in winter vegetable production, freshwater shrimp farming, and king crab production.

Africa

In the African region south of the Sahara Desert, the Peace Corps assists in food production, water-resource development, and developing sources of energy. Many volunteers continue to work in education projects, although the emphasis is now on training teachers and teaching vocational skills. The corps also works to develop the economy and upgrade the quality of health care. The Peace Corps places about half of its volunteers in the 27 African nations it serves. The nations with the largest number of volunteers are Sierra Leone, Kenya, Botswana, and Zaire.

One special Peace Corps project is the Africa Food Systems Initiative, created in 1985 to alleviate a severe food crisis caused by famine. A 10-year effort in cooperation with AID and the World Bank (an international agency that lends money for development), the initiative began with pilot programs in Mali, Niger, Zaire, and Lesotho. Since then, four more countries—Senegal, Guinea, the Central African Republic, and Sierra Leone—have been added. The Peace Corps plans to add another four by 1990. In these countries, the corps helps to improve irrigation systems, introduces farmers to the use of oxen, and increases the production of fertilizers to produce more food. Individual volunteers are starting vegetable gardens and fish-farming projects and improving food crops and planting methods.

Peace Corps achievements in Africa include a project in Mali in which volunteers built 13 wells and trained local artisans in well construction. More than a dozen additional volunteers worked in 30 nurseries, planting thousands of trees and training Malians in forestry.

Shaded areas represent Peace Corps host countries in the African region, 1961–89.

Florida native Eric Breidenbach encourages villagers in the Tillabery region of Niger to build and use three-rock mud stoves, which consume little fuel and thus conserve scarce firewood. Breidenbach works on various projects in the region, from fisheries to tree planting.

In Niger, volunteers taught 1,000 villagers to make adobe stoves that use less wood to cook food and educated them on the dangers of desertification (the growth of the desert). Volunteers also trained 1,500 young people and women to make handicrafts they could sell, taught home economics, and taught physical education.

Volunteers in Liberia helped that country establish its first national wildlife park, Sapo National Park. They helped Liberians plant exotic and native plants and promoted programs in conservation. And in Mauritania, Peace Corps workers planted trees as wind breakers and started fruit-tree plantations. Health volunteers there supervised 25 community feeding centers for malnourished children.

These programs have not revolutionized the developing world. Not all Peace Corps projects have been as successful as the ones cited. Yet, little by little, project by project, the corps has made tiny inroads in development. Over the years the agency has been wearing away at the stubborn problems of hunger, disease, poverty, and illiteracy that continue to plague the developing nations in the Third World. At the same time, the corps has inspired an understanding and a spirit of international cooperation among individuals.

Peace Corps service offers both challenges and rewards. Two of the most important qualities a volunteer must have are an openness to other cultures and a strong motivation and commitment to the work of the Peace Corps.

SIX

The Men and Women of the Peace Corps

On television and radio stations, singer-entertainer Harry Belafonte's velvety voice invites people to join the Peace Corps, "the toughest job you'll ever love." Most recruiting for the agency, however, is done on college campuses around the country. The corps also advertises in local newspapers and in magazines. To attract minorities and older applicants, the agency targets black and retirement publications in its advertising campaign.

Prospective volunteers must first fill out an application telling about their background, schooling, interests, and talents. Volunteers must be at least 18 years old and United States citizens. (There is no upper age limit for Peace Corps service.) Applicants must also have no legal or medical problems. Married volunteers are required to serve with their spouses and are rarely accepted for Peace Corps service if they have dependent children.

Applicants are interviewed by a recruiter to assess their level of commitment to the work. Recruiters must also discern the applicants' sensitivity to other cultures and receptivity to new and different experiences. Applicants are asked if they have any training in a special area such as speech therapy, medical technology, or civil engineering; recruits with none of these skills but a liberal-arts degree are questioned about their other interests to see if these skills can be used by the Peace Corps.

Horticulture extension volunteers Lee and Karen Altier advise a Nepali farmer on crop production. Married Peace Corps volunteers are required to serve with their spouses.

Recruiters will look for ways to match each recruit's educational background and interests to the skills host countries have requested. For instance, one particular applicant may be a liberal-arts graduate—as are more than 20 percent of applicants. But she keeps a tank of tropical fish and took college courses in biology and chemistry. This is an interest the Peace Corps can use as the basis for further special training. With her interest in fish culture and her science courses, the recruit can be trained in fish farming and taught to assist farmers in developing and stocking man-made fish ponds. If the applicant had a degree in biology or work experience in a clinic, she could be trained to do health and nutrition work. For example, she could be taught cardiopulmonary resuscitation (CPR) and assigned to lead seminars in her host country.

Most of the men and women who are accepted as volunteers have a skill that can be utilized by the corps: 31 percent have professional skills in business, engineering, health care, or social work; 28 percent are skilled in education; 15 percent in agriculture; and 4 percent in trades, such as carpenters, electricians, masons, or welders.

The volunteer recruitment section of the Peace Corps's placement office puts out a list of positions available overseas. Recruiters who are satisfied with an applicant's qualifications will recommend him or her for a specific position in the corps. Recruits next must take a medical examination and gather eight letters of recommendation from friends, employers, and teachers. The application and the recommendation letters are sent to the nearest of three regional centers—either Chicago, New York, or San Francisco—for a first review. If the regional center approves the application, it forwards it to the

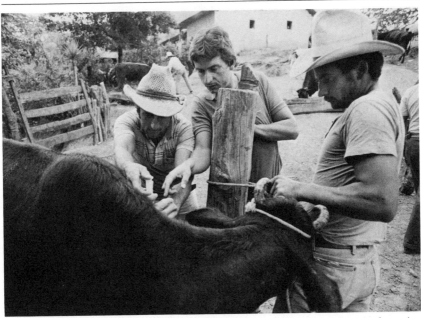

Volunteer Ray Archuleta (center) works for a local ministry of agriculture in a village in Guatemala. Peace Corps recruiters matched Archuleta's interest in agriculture and his experience in the U.S. Forest Service to place him in this position.

placement office at headquarters. The recruit's medical records are sent to the medical division for clearance.

After a second review, the placement office formally offers placement as a Peace Corps volunteer. The recruit must now wait for information on his or her host country and details on training. Each recruit reports to a staging site for a short orientation to the Peace Corps and the host country that lasts from three and one-half to eight days. Recruits also receive vaccinations against diseases such as typhoid. For the third time, their motivation and commitment are evaluated. About five percent of trainees leave the agency after the staging.

Trainees now begin studying their special-skill projects. U.S.-based training classes for generalists include fish farming, forestry, vegetable gardening, beekeeping, and small-animal breeding. After completing this course of training, recruits are sent overseas to their host countries.

Agriculture trainees learn about plant diseases at a Peace Corps training site near San Jose, Costa Rica, in 1985. Increased satisfaction with the corps's training program in the 1980s led to fewer volunteers leaving their posts before completing their two years of service.

In the early days of the Peace Corps, training was measurably different. Every volunteer had to take courses in his or her host country's language, anthropology, and economics from professors in American universities. They were then sent to a training camp in Puerto Rico or Hawaii for strenuous physical fitness training, including a four-day survival trek.

The Peace Corps says its training in the 1980s has evolved to be "less optimistic and more realistic." It is also less physically demanding. The corps works hard to tailor each volunteer's training to the needs of his or her particular assignment. Much of the training today in language and culture is taught by former volunteers or host-country nationals, and classes are held in the country of assignment. One measure of the success of this strategy is the reduction in the number of volunteers who drop out of the corps and leave their projects: In the 1970s, more than 30 percent of volunteers left before their 2 years of service were finished; in the 1980s, that number dropped to nearly 20 percent. About 15 percent of volunteers opt to serve a third year on their assignment.

The support staff in the overseas offices arranges to continue the volunteers' training in the foreign language of the country, local customs, and additional skills. In addition to their primary assignments, volunteers are encouraged to take on second or even third projects. Secondary assignments might include such activities as starting vegetable gardens, raising chickens, building toilets, or constructing fuel-saving stoves. The beginning volunteers are also taught to be sensitive to the customs of their host countries. They learn about traditional foods, dress, and some important taboos. Volunteers are taught that in some cultures people are affronted if one shakes their hand, touches them, or eats or offers gifts with the left hand.

The training stage in the host country lasts from 8 to 14 weeks. When it is over, volunteers must pass a test to show that they can communicate in the host country's language. Now full-fledged Peace Corps volunteers, they are taken to their posts to begin work on their projects. The entire process, from the time a recruit first applies until the time he or she begins a 24-month tour of duty, takes between 6 and 9 months.

The Peace Corps gives its volunteers an allowance to pay for food, housing, clothing, transportation, and other living expenses. The amount each receives depends on costs in his or her host country. At the same time, the Peace Corps puts aside $200 per month for each volunteer to receive when he or she finishes the tour of duty.

Volunteers regularly visit the Peace Corps's offices in their host countries to get mail, obtain any medical treatment they may need, and discuss the progress of their projects. Each volunteer is allowed to take up to 48 days of vacation time during the 24-month tour of duty to travel in the host country and the surrounding areas. The Peace Corps finances this vacation by setting aside $24 per month of service per volunteer.

Minorities in the Peace Corps

Volunteer ranks are equally divided between men and women. Despite the equal representation between the sexes, most volunteers are white. The corps has tried for years to increase the number of minority volunteers, with limited success. In 1988, only five percent of Peace Corps volunteers were black or Hispanic.

The corps has taken several different approaches to attract more minorities to its ranks. Career goals are often a top priority for minority college graduates, many of whom have traditionally been at an economic disadvantage. Many blacks and Hispanics have said that they fear they will lose two years of work experience if they join the Peace Corps. To aid in minority recruitment, the agency must convince potential candidates that special advantages and opportunities offset any time loss. In recent years, the corps has sponsored forums and discussions in conjunction with local minority organizations to get the message out that serving as a volunteer can help on the career ladder. The agency points out that a recent study showed that former Peace Corps volunteers outperform fellow workers in such areas as promotions and salary increases. Peace Corps veterans also have an advantage when they apply for jobs with the federal government. And many corporations look favorably on hiring former volunteers.

Another strategy the Peace Corps has developed to attract minorities is to offer a program of combined service and graduate study. Two schools, the University of South Carolina and the University of Alabama, have programs under which minority graduate students may become volunteers after one year of study and receive college credit for the time they spend abroad.

Some notable black Peace Corps veterans are Dr. Carolyn Payton, the first black woman Peace Corps director; Franklin Williams, a civil rights attorney who accompanied Sargent Shriver on his first trip around the world to set up the program; and Vinette Jones, who served as director of recruitment, one of the three major units within the Peace Corps, in the 1980s.

Another notable black corpsman is Martin Puryear, who served as a volunteer from 1964 to 1966. Puryear spent two years teaching in a mission school in Sierra Leone. A successful painter before he joined the corps, in

Mark White (right) teaches math and science at the College of Commerce in Bamenda, Cameroon. Although the Peace Corps has developed many strategies to encourage minority participation, only about five percent of volunteers are minorities.

Africa, Puryear got to know a local carpenter who made what Puryear described as incredible wooden furniture. Puryear later said he had never thought of working in wood as a way of making art before that experience. Today, Puryear's wood carvings make him one of America's foremost contemporary sculptors.

Dana Hallman, a young black woman who served as a Peace Corps volunteer, was stationed in Tanzania from 1983 to 1985. She joined the corps after graduating from Hofstra University in New York with a liberal-arts degree. Because of Hallman's interest in gardening, the Peace Corps trained her as an agriculture extension worker. After six weeks of agricultural training at an institute in the United States, Hallman went to her post, where further agricultural training was supplemented by lessons in Swahili, the country's language.

Hallman was sent to a small, remote village. The nearest volunteer was three and one-half hours away by motorcycle. In her little house, Hallman felt isolated and lonely—a feeling common to many volunteers for the first few months of an assignment. She credits the women of the village for teaching her basic survival—how to light her coal stove; how to get clean water. They literally took her by the hand to market to shop for food.

"It was a slow integrative process but the people were incredible," says Hallman. Even though there were many people around her, Hallman still felt lonely. She wrote many letters home, read a lot, and visited the nearest volunteer every month. After the first six to nine months, her loneliness faded as she became fluent in Swahili and the last barriers to communication ended.

However, it took Hallman even longer to be fully accepted as an agricultural worker. When she came to the village, the farmers were accustomed to planting their crops by scattering seed haphazardly over the ground. They scoffed at Hallman's more sophisticated planting methods.

"Being an American, they didn't think I could grow anything," she recalled. "So I planted a demonstration plot. The people laughed because they had never seen anyone plant corn and beans in rows." When the corn plants started to grow, however, attitudes in the village began to change. "When the corn hit three feet, people started knocking on my door, asking me how I did it," Hallman later said.

What really broke the ice for Hallman was the Swiss chard that she grew in her vegetable garden. The local people loved the taste of the vegetable and came to her to get seeds to grow it themselves. "I'm convinced that the Swiss chard is still growing there," she said. "I didn't effect major change. But the friends I made, I'm still in touch with and I learned a lot about life in the developing world."

Older Volunteers

As a young college graduate, Dana Hallman typifies the average American's idea of a Peace Corps volunteer. But gradually over the years, as the agency came to stress experience and skills for its representatives, the average age of volunteers rose from 24 in the 1960s to 30 in the 1980s.

Today's Peace Corps actively courts older Americans—even senior citizens—to become volunteers. These people offer accumulated life experiences and skills that can benefit programs in developing nations in many ways. In 1962 only 3 percent, or 82 volunteers, were more than 50 years old; in 1988, however, 11 percent of Peace Corps volunteers were older than 50.

The agency has found that older volunteers are dedicated workers, relate well to people, and enjoy a special place of honor in Third World nations

Senior volunteer Odilon Long (left) supervises roof construction at Bunumbu Teachers College in Sierra Leone in 1980. Long worked as a designer and technical adviser for school and other construction projects from 1967 to 1987.

because of their age. One of the prize examples of a successful senior Peace Corps volunteer is Odilon Long, a retired worker for Illinois Bell Telephone. On March 1, 1967, the same day he left the telephone company after 41 years, Long joined the Peace Corps and started a whole new life.

Long was born in a logging town near Canada and spoke only French until he was 18, so the corps sent him to French-speaking West Africa. For the next 16 years, he worked as a designer and technical adviser on the construction of schools, roads, and bridges in the Ivory Coast, Gabon, Togo, Sierra Leone, and Burkina Faso. One of his favorite assignments was in Sierra Leone, where he helped relocate a school building to a larger site. When he finally left Africa, Long signed up to serve in Haiti. "When you have idle moments, when your mind is not occupied, you start feeling your age," he said. "I don't have idle moments." After almost 20 years of service, Long left the corps in 1987 at age 85. He held the double record of being both the oldest and the longest-serving volunteer.

While not every older volunteer's service in the Peace Corps is as spectacular as Long's, many have found the adventure and challenge a worthwhile experience. The agency has made certain accommodations to lure these Americans into becoming volunteers, such as allowing them a longer time to arrange affairs before departure to the host country; varying the length of assignment for those who cannot serve the full two years; and experimenting with new methods to teach the necessary foreign languages.

Life in the Peace Corps

Many Peace Corps volunteers have learned the wisdom of the saying, Make haste slowly. It is only with patience and understanding that people gradually come to accept the changes volunteers have to offer. One volunteer reported that it took her a year of living with a family to convince them to boil their drinking water the necessary 20 minutes to kill all the bacteria. With her persistent example, day after day, they finally changed.

Every volunteer has to find his or her own way to overcome this resistance to change. Harriet Lesser, who served as a volunteer teacher in Nigeria from 1964 to 1966, was put to the test almost immediately after she began her assignment. Her battle was to overcome the rigid educational system that prevailed at the Government Technical Institute, where she taught.

Lesser's class of teenage boys, 16 to 18 years old, was preparing to take a major exam that could win them jobs with the government or places at the

Famous Artist
and Still Paint
Pictures

Presentation & Signing
Saturday, January 25th • 2:00 p.m.

Barnes & Noble
Booksellers *Since 1873*

818 South Rd.
(914) 297-8092

Simon & Schuster

Children's

Ordering: 1800-223
2 336

Lights, Camera, Action
Beth Cruise

ISBN: 0689 718861

Special order — Natalie

university. There was enormous pressure on these students to do well. In this school, as in many in Africa, rote memorization was the basis of teaching. The teacher would write things on the board, and the class would copy them down and learn them by heart. What they did not learn to do was to analyze, discuss, or question. Their ability to reason, to think, or to reach their own conclusions was not part of the curriculum.

When Lesser tried to change the method of teaching, her class rebelled. "I had a riot in my classroom," she later said. They were arguing and yelling and some refused to stay in the class—leaving by the windows as well as the door. When she finally managed to get the class quieted down, Lesser made them a promise. "I told them, if they stayed with me, they would learn better than before—that I was teaching them to think."

Lesser completely won them over six months later when she prepared them to debate with a girls' school down the road. They did well in the debate and afterward went to a dance with the other students. "After that I felt they would follow me anywhere," she said. When the time came for them to take their exams, her students ended up doing better than any other class in the previous five years.

Lesser was faced with many other challenges, including living with no refrigerator, washing clothes in a bathtub, and relying on a wood stove as her only source of heat. But she has never doubted that her experience was worthwhile. More than 20 years later, she claimed that the experience changed her life forever; she called it "a lesson in international relations on an intimate level—learning to make yourself understood to someone completely different from you."

The Returning Volunteer

The Peace Corps now proudly claims more than 120,000 alumni. Every state, plus Puerto Rico, Guam, the Virgin Islands, and the Panama Canal Zone, has provided the corps with volunteers and staff. California and New York have the most former Peace Corps workers (16,000 and 11,000, respectively), followed by Illinois, Pennsylvania, Massachusetts, Michigan, Ohio, and Colorado.

Many alumni have gone on to notable careers in government service, education, business, journalism, and other prestigious fields. The U.S. Senate has had three members who served in the Peace Corps: Christopher Dodd of Connecticut (volunteer, Dominican Republic, 1966–68; U.S. senator 1981–), Paul Tsongas of Massachusetts (volunteer, Ethiopia, 1962–64; U.S. senator

*Former U.S. senator Paul Tsongas of Massachusetts (1979–85) was a Peace
Corps volunteer in Ethiopia from 1962 to 1964. Although he later served successful terms in the Senate and the House of Representatives, Tsongas
claimed, "I've never done anything as important in my life as the two years in
the Peace Corps."*

1979–85), and Alan Cranston of California (Peace Corps staff, Ghana, 1965;
U.S. senator 1969–   ). In 1988, seven members of the House of Representatives were Peace Corps veterans.

Many former volunteers serve throughout the federal and state governments. Peace Corps veterans serve in state legislatures in Oklahoma,

California, Massachusetts, and Pennsylvania. Ten percent of people entering the Foreign Service are former volunteers, and more than 500 Peace Corps alumni have continued to serve the people of the Third World by working for AID. The former head of this development agency, Peter McPherson, who was a Peace Corps volunteer in Peru from 1964 to 1966, went on to be deputy treasury secretary in the Reagan administration.

The field of education has many successful Peace Corps alumni, including Donna Shalala, chancellor of the University of Wisconsin, and Allan Fuskin, president of Antioch University in Ohio. In communications, former volunteers are working as reporters and editors at the *Wall Street Journal*, the *Washington Post*, the *San Francisco Examiner*, the *New York Daily News*, and *Time* magazine.

The financial and business worlds claim Peace Corps veterans as well: More than 35 top Chase Manhattan Bank financial officers are former volunteers, as

Michael B. McCaskey, who served as a Peace Corps volunteer in Fiche, Ethiopia, from 1965 to 1967, was named president of the Chicago Bears football team in 1983. McCaskey maintains, "Peace Corps really is 'the toughest job you'll ever love,' but if you're willing to accept the challenge and make the run, the touchdown score is much more than six points."

109

A former Peace Corps volunteer reads a passage from his journal at the 1988 vigil in the U.S. Capitol to commemorate the 25th anniversary of President Kennedy's assassination. Returned volunteers constitute a valuable resource for Peace Corps planners and foreign-service agencies.

is Robert Haas, president of the Levi Strauss clothing firm. These names are the most visible of the thousands of Peace Corps alumni; others are teachers, social workers, engineers, business people, nurses, and other successful members of American society.

To help returning volunteers along the path to career success, the corps offers career counseling and publishes a bulletin called the "Job Hotline." In addition, the federal government gives former volunteers special eligibility for federal civil service jobs and forgives a portion of the debt on student loans they have taken through the National Direct Student Loan program.

The academic community also recognizes former volunteers' hard work and accomplishments by offering Peace Corps alumni more than 100 university scholarships, grants, and work-study positions. Many graduate schools offer academic credit for Peace Corps service as well.

Returning volunteers are also eligible to join the National Council of Returned Peace Corps Volunteers. This group of former volunteers has a membership of more than 5,200 and works to make sure that the Peace Corps's goal of promoting mutual understanding between the United States and developing nations is fulfilled. Timothy Carroll, the group's executive director, says the council wants to educate Americans about the needs of the Third World and lobby Congress for more humane and effective foreign aid. The council also acts as an advocate for the Peace Corps and seeks to strengthen its budget.

The council sponsors annual conferences for returning volunteers. The conferences feature job fairs, workshops, and panels on development issues. They also allow members to socialize. In 1988, on the 25th anniversary of President Kennedy's assassination, the council sponsored a 24-hour vigil at the Capitol. To honor the memory of the Peace Corps's founder, returned volunteers from across the country took turns reading three-minute passages from their journals on what the overseas experience meant to them.

Peace Corps volunteers supervise citrus-seed planting at the AID-funded Bandiagara Tree Nursery in Mali. Cooperation with AID and other development agencies has allowed the corps to increase the impact and scope of its programs.

SEVEN

The Peace Corps in the Future

Under Director Loret Ruppe's leadership in the 1980s, the Peace Corps moved forcefully in several directions to meet the complex needs of the developing world. Congress underscored this effort by recommending that the number of volunteers be increased to 10,000 per year by the early 1990s. It also modified the 5-year service rule so that 15 percent of the staff could stay an extra 2½ years, thus reducing the loss of experienced personnel.

At the same time, the corps put a new emphasis on cooperation with other federal agencies and private voluntary organizations in order to increase the impact of its projects. In addition to its many projects in conjunction with AID, the Peace Corps works with international development agencies such as the World Bank, the United Nations International Children's Education Fund (UNICEF), and the World Health Organization. The U.S. Departments of Agriculture, Commerce, and State work with the Peace Corps, as do private voluntary organizations such as Catholic Relief Services and Project Hope. The Peace Corps also coordinates its projects with voluntary organizations in Canada, Germany, Great Britain, Sweden, and Switzerland.

Besides working in conjunction with other groups, the Peace Corps has taken steps to widen its base of support among the American public. In 1985, Congress created a permanent Peace Corps National Advisory Council, a

15-member committee appointed by the president that advises the Peace Corps leadership on policies and programs and thus increases involvement and interest in its operations. Ruppe also put new emphasis on public involvement in the Peace Corps by reviving the Partnership Program, a project created in 1964 to reach out to the business community and the American public for financial help to bring development to the Third World. The Partnership Program allows Americans to directly assist individual Peace Corps projects through small-scale fund-raising. Small investments can start many community projects and fund businessmen such as shoemakers, carpenters, and grocers. From 1964 to the 1980s, the Partnership Program raised a total of $3 million for more than 2,000 self-help projects in 90 developing countries.

Another way the Peace Corps reaches out to increase the effects of its work is by supporting the United Nations Volunteer (UNV) program, an international organization based on the Peace Corps and similar groups that was created in 1970. UNVs are recruited from all UN member nations and serve in development projects designed by UN agencies such as UNICEF and the World Food Organization. Besides recruiting Americans for the Geneva-based organization, the Peace Corps pays for their transportation and resettlement expenses. Most Americans who become UNVs are former Peace Corps volunteers; sometimes, these returned Peace Corps volunteers are assigned to serve in countries where the Peace Corps has no programs, such as Chad, Uganda, and Zimbabwe.

The Peace Corps has moved to strengthen its ties with American colleges and universities as well. Recently, the corps announced joint programs with schools such as Boston University, the University of Alabama, Yale University, Rutgers University, Harvard University, Colorado State University, and the University of South Carolina. The agency hopes that this move will yield a more qualified volunteer and at the same time provide graduate students with invaluable field experience.

Public health graduate students from Boston University and the University of Alabama may serve as Peace Corps volunteers under a program that will help them complete their master's degrees. Agriculture and forestry students from Colorado State University and Yale University can also earn graduate credit by serving as volunteers. And Harvard's fifth-year dental students can elect to serve six-month terms as volunteers in rural Jamaica, where they will provide training and dental care.

Shortening the 24-month tour of duty is another move the Peace Corps has undertaken to attract more professionals to the agency. The new Associate Volunteer program allows professionals such as teachers, doctors, nurses,

The person-to-person orientation of the Peace Corps's programs nurtures a spirit of international cooperation and mutual understanding.

veterinarians, and businesspeople to work in developing countries for tours lasting from 3 to 15 months. In the late 1980s, for example, the corps looked for dentists willing to serve six months in the Marshall islands and math and science teachers for teacher-training projects in Belize.

The Peace Corps was founded on the simple idea of people helping people—of Swiss chard growing in Tanzania, of newly planted trees in Nepal, and of oxen pulling plows in Togo. It is a story of Americans in remote villages far from home conquering feelings of loneliness and isolation to share their knowledge with others. In a speech on November 2, 1960, John F. Kennedy addressed the essence of the Peace Corps:

> There is not enough money in all America to relieve the misery of the underdeveloped world in a giant and endless soup kitchen. But there is enough know-how and enough knowledgeable people to help those nations help themselves.

Kennedy knew that in addition to leaving behind the actual projects they had helped create, Peace Corps workers left individuals in developing nations with the precious knowledge that they could effect change themselves. The president established the Peace Corps in 1961 to channel American energy toward helping end poverty, disease, and misery in less-developed nations around the world. More than a quarter of a century later—as television and newspapers constantly remind us—the needs of poor people in developing countries remain as compelling as they did when the Peace Corps was first formed.

Peace Corps

```
                        ┌──────────┐
                        │ DIRECTOR │
                        └────┬─────┘         ┌─────────────────────┐
                             │               │ EXECUTIVE SECRETARIAT │
                             │               └─────────────────────┘
   ┌─────────┬───────────────┼───────────────┬──────────┐
┌──────────┐ ┌──────────────┐ ┌──────────────┐ ┌──────────┐
│ GENERAL  │ │ PRIVATE SECTOR│ │ CONGRESSIONAL│ │ PUBLIC   │
│ COUNSEL  │ │ DEVELOPMENT  │ │ RELATIONS    │ │ AFFAIRS  │
└──────────┘ └──────────────┘ └──────────────┘ └──────────┘
```

INTERNATIONAL OPERATIONS	MANAGEMENT	VOLUNTEER RECRUITMENT AND SELECTION
AFRICA OPERATIONS	MEDICAL SERVICES	MARKETING
INTER–AMERICA OPERATIONS	SPECIAL SERVICES	RECRUITMENT
NANEAP OPERATIONS	PERSONNEL POLICY AND OPERATIONS	PLACEMENT
TRAINING AND PROGRAM SUPPORT	FINANCIAL MANAGEMENT	STAGING
OVERSEAS POSTS	PLANNING AND POLICY ANALYSIS	
	ADMINISTRATIVE SERVICES	
	COMPLIANCE	
	INFORMATION RESOURCES MANAGEMENT	

117

GLOSSARY

Beriberi   A deficiency disease marked by inflammatory or degenerative changes of the nerves, digestive system, and heart and caused by a lack of vitamin B_1, or thiamine.

Cold war   A conflict over ideological differences that leads to rivalry, mistrust, and often open hostility short of violence between two nations or groups of nations. Despite the conflict between the nations, diplomatic relations are usually maintained.

Draft   A system for selecting individuals from a group for mandatory military service.

Generalist   A term used to describe a Peace Corps volunteer who has a liberal arts degree rather than training in a specific field such as biology.

Humanitarian   A person who promotes human welfare and social reform.

Leprosy   A chronic, infectious disease, occurring almost exclusively in tropical and subtropical regions, that can lead to disfigurement and the loss of limbs.

Malaria   An infectious disease characterized by cycles of chills, fever, and sweating and transmitted by the bite of the infected female anopheles mosquito.

Missionary   A person sent to perform a humanitarian service in a foreign country.

Specialist   A Peace Corps volunteer who has special skills and training in a particular area such as agriculture or medicine.

Third World   A term used to describe the group of underdeveloped nations of the world.

Tilapia   African freshwater food fish.

Tuberculosis   A contagious disease of man and certain other vertebrates caused by a microorganism and manifesting itself in lesions on the lungs, bones, and other parts of the body.

SELECTED REFERENCES

Ashabranner, Brent. *A Moment in History: The First Ten Years of the Peace Corps.* Garden City, NY: Doubleday, 1971.

Carter, Lillian, and Gloria Carter Spann. *Away from Home: Letters to My Family.* New York: Simon & Schuster, 1977.

Dolezal, Suzanne. "Kennedy's Kids Grow Up." *Detroit Free Press,* November 20, 1983.

Ezickson, Aaron J., ed. *The Peace Corps: A Pictorial History.* New York: Hill & Wang, 1965.

Fuchs, Lawrence H. *Those Peculiar Americans: The Peace Corps and American National Character.* New York: Meredith, 1967.

Hapgood, David, and Meridan Bennett. *Agents of Change: A Close Look at the Peace Corps.* Boston: Little, Brown, 1986.

Levitt, Leonard. *An African Season.* New York: Simon & Schuster, 1967.

Lowther, Kevin, and C. Payne Lucas. *Keeping Kennedy's Promise: The Peace Corps, Unmet Hope of the New Frontier.* Boulder, CO: Westview, 1978.

Madow, Pauline. *The Peace Corps.* New York: H. W. Wilson, 1964.

Peace Corps. *The Peace Corps in the Eighties.* Washington, DC: Peace Corps, 1987.

————. *Peace Corps Times.* Washington, DC: Peace Corps, 1978–.

————. *Twenty Years of Peace Corps.* Washington, DC: Peace Corps, 1981.

Redmon, Coates. *Come as You Are: The Peace Corps Story.* San Diego: Harcourt Brace Jovanovich, 1986.

Rice, Gerard T. *The Bold Experiment: JFK's Peace Corps.* Notre Dame, IN: University of Notre Dame Press, 1985.

Sanders, Geneva. *The Gringo Brought His Mother: A Peace Corps Adventure with a Difference.* San Antonio: Corona Publishing, 1986.

Shriver, Sargent. *Point of the Lance.* New York: Harper & Row, 1964.

Shute, Nancy. "After a Turbulent Youth, the Peace Corps Comes of Age." *Smithsonian,* February 1986, 81–89.

Viorst, Milton, ed. *Making a Difference: The Peace Corps at Twenty-five.* New York: Weidenfeld and Nicholson, 1986.

INDEX

ACCION, 59
ACTION, 63, 64, 66, 68, 72, 73
Active Corps of Executives
  (ACE), 63
Afghanistan, 29, 50, 71
Africa, 15, 18, 21, 22, 23, 27,
  34, 42, 46, 50, 51, 53, 68, 74,
  85, 86, 93, 95, 106
Africa Food Systems Initiative,
  74, 93
Agency for International Devel-
  opment (AID), 40, 75, 82,
  93, 109, 113
Agriculture, 22, 27, 50, 54, 68,
  80, 82, 87, 92, 99, 103
  U.S. Department of, 113
Alliance for Progress, 35
American Friends Service Com-
  mittee, 24
Ashabranner, Brent, 47, 48, 54
Asia, 15, 18, 21, 27, 34, 35, 42,
  50, 53, 56, 67, 90
Associate Volunteer program,
  114–15

Bangladesh, 68, 71
Barbados, 63, 67
Belize, 93, 116
Beriberi, 24, 25
Blatchford, Joseph H., 59, 60,
  61, 62, 63, 64
Botswana, 53, 93
Bowles, Chester, 42
Brazil, 67, 76, 77
Brown, Samuel W., Jr., 66, 67,
  68, 71
Buxton, Thomas Fowell, 22, 23

Cambodia, 29, 31
Caribbean, 66, 74, 82, 92, 93
Caribbean Basin Initiative, 74,
  92

Carroll, Timothy, 111
Carter, Jimmy, 65, 66, 67, 68,
  72
Carter, Lillian, 66
Catholicism, 21, 24, 27
Catholic Relief Services, 113
Celeste, Richard, 68, 71
Central African Republic, 81,
  93
Central America, 15, 74, 92
Central Intelligence Agency, 43
Chad, 53, 71, 114
Chile, 44, 54, 57, 67, 76
Christian Missionary Society,
  22
Church World Service, 24
Civilian Conservation Corps
  (CCC), 30
Colombia, 44, 54, 71, 76
Commerce, U.S. Department of,
  113
Communism, 15, 36, 56
Competitive Enterprise
  Development, 73
Congress, U.S., 16, 31–33, 45,
  52, 57, 64, 68, 73, 77, 111,
  113
Costa Rica, 67, 92, 93
Cranston, Alan, 108

Deliver Us From Evil (Dooley),
  28
Dellenback, John, 64
Disease, 24, 82, 84, 100
Dodd, Christopher, 107
Dominican Republic, 45, 50, 87,
  107
Dooley, Thomas, 27–29, 35

Education, 18, 23, 25, 26, 36,
  47, 50, 55, 59, 68, 80–82, 87,
  90, 93, 95, 99, 109

Eisenhower, Dwight D., 40, 49, 59
El Salvador, 71, 76
Engineering, 18, 54, 81, 99

"First Peace Corps," 24–26
Fisheries, 80, 84–85, 98, 100
Ford, Gerald, 64
Foreign Service, 32, 43
Forestry, 18, 54, 80, 85, 90, 93, 100
Foster Grandparent Program (FGP), 63
Fuskin, Allan, 109

Ghana, 34, 43, 44, 47, 50
Great Britain, 113
Great Depression, 29
Guam, 24, 107
Guatemala, 92, 93
Guinea, 63, 93

Haas, Robert, 100
Haiti, 29, 106
Hallman, Dana, 103–4
Health care, 18, 50, 54, 71, 80, 82, 84, 87, 93, 99
Heiser, Victor, 24
Honduras, 92, 93
Humphrey, Hubert, 32, 34, 37, 45

India, 43, 54, 66, 67, 71, 77
Information Collection and Exchange (ICE), 64
Initiative for Central America, 74, 93
Inter-America, 92–93
Interior, U.S. Department of the, 26
International Cooperation Administration, 40, 53
International Voluntary Services (IVS), 26–27, 32
Ivory Coast, 50, 76, 106

Johnson, Lyndon B., 32, 40, 43, 51, 53, 56, 59, 63, 65
Jones, Vinette, 102
Josephson, William, 39, 40, 41

Kaunda, Kenneth, 24
Kennedy, John F., 15, 16, 32, 33, 34, 35, 36, 40, 42, 43, 45, 46, 50, 51, 59, 65, 68, 72, 77, 116
Kenya, 24, 86, 93
Kenyatta, Jomo, 23
Korea, 67. See also South Korea

Laos, 28, 29, 35
Latin America, 18, 21, 34, 35, 50, 53, 59, 67
Leprosy, 24
Lesser, Harriet, 106, 107
Libya, 53, 63
Loff, Debbie, 71
Long, Odilon, 106

McPherson, Peter, 75, 109
Malaria, 23, 86
Malaysia, 67, 76
Mali, 43, 93
Mauritania, 53, 63, 95
Medical International Cooperation (MEDICO), 29
Michelmore, Margery, 48, 49
Micronesia, 53, 54, 82
Middle East, 21, 27
Missionaries, 21, 22, 23–24, 27
Morocco, 68, 87
Moyers, Bill, 40, 41, 43
Murray, Bruce, 57

National Council of Returned Peace Corps Volunteeers, 110–11
National Lutheran Council, 24
National Youth Administration (NYA), 30
Near East, 87

Nepal, 50, 90, 116
Niger, 93, 95
Nigeria, 22, 47, 48, 49, 50, 106
Nixon, Richard M., 34, 59, 62, 63, 71
Nkrumah, Kwame, 43
North Africa, the Near East, Asia, and the Pacific Islands (NANEAP), 87–92
North Vietnam, 28, 56, 57
Nutrition, 18, 71, 80, 82, 84, 93, 99
Nyerere, Julius, 24

Office of Economic Opportunity, 53

Pacific Islands, 18, 90, 92
Pakistan, 43, 50, 63, 71, 77
Panama, 53, 107
Partnership Program, 114
Passman, Otto, 63
Pauken, Thomas, 73
Payton, Carolyn R., 66–67, 68, 102
Peace Corps
  under Carter administration, 65–72
  congressional support for, 31–33
  established, 16, 37
  field projects, 80–87
  under Ford administration, 64–65
  funding for, 52, 63, 65, 76, 77
  future of, 113–16
  goals of, 18
  host countries of, 87–95
  under Johnson administration, 51–55
  minorities in, 102–4
  models for, 21–33
  under Nixon administration, 59–64, 71
  under Reagan administration, 72–77

recruitment for, 97–107
reorganization of, 63–64
skepticism about, 42–44
staffing of, 39–40, 45, 52, 79
during Vietnam War, 55–57, 62, 72
volunteer training, 18, 54, 65, 72, 100–101
Peace Corps Act, 45, 71
Peace Corps National Advisory Council, 113–14
Peru, 29, 109
Philippines, 24, 26, 44, 50, 54, 55, 67, 82, 86, 87, 90
Point Four Youth Corps, 31
Project Hope, 113
Protestantism, 21, 24, 27
Puerto Rico, 24, 107
Puryear, Martin, 102–3

Reagan, Ronald, 72, 109
Retired Senior Volunteer Program (RSVP), 63
Reuss, Henry, 31, 32, 33, 34, 37, 45
Rogers, William, 62
Roosevelt, Franklin D., 29, 30, 31
Ruppe, Loret Miller, 72–77, 80, 113, 114
Rusk, Dean, 42

St. Lucia, 44, 50, 63
Salinger, Pierre, 35
Sanitation projects, 80, 85–86
Senegal, 67, 93
Service Corps of Retired Executives (SCORE), 63
Shalala, Donna, 109
Shriver, R. Sargent, 37, 39, 41, 42, 43, 45, 46, 52, 53, 61, 72, 74, 77, 102
Sierra Leone, 93, 102, 106
Slavery, 21–22
Small-business development, 18, 71, 73, 74, 80, 87, 90, 92

123

Somalia, 63
Sorensen, Theodore, 35
South America, 15, 21, 50, 59, 92
South Korea, 53, 67, 71, 76
South Vietnam, 28, 56
Spain, 24, 26
Starr, Dick, 71
State, U.S. Department of, 42, 45, 56, 113
Sweden, 26, 113

Tanzania, 24, 44, 46, 50, 63, 103, 116
Thailand, 63, 86, 87, 90
Third World, 15, 16, 26, 35, 36, 40, 42, 50, 53, 54, 57, 60, 67, 71, 73, 77, 81, 82, 84, 85, 87, 95, 104, 109, 111, 114
Togo, 82, 106, 116
"Towering Task, The," 41
Truman, Harry S., 31
Tsongas, Paul, 107
Turkey, 43, 50

Ugly American, The (Burdick and Lederer), 27
United Nations Educational, Scientific, and Cultural Organization (UNESCO), 21, 31
United Nations International Children's Education Fund (UNICEF), 113, 114
United Nations Volunteer program, 114

United States, 16, 24, 25, 27, 28, 29, 34, 35, 36, 42, 45, 56, 87

Vaughn, Jack Hook, 53, 54, 57, 61
Vietnam, 27, 31, 73. See also North Vietnam; South Vietnam
Vietnam War, 55, 56, 57, 62, 66, 72
Volunteers
    minority, 102–4
    older, 104–6
    recruitment of, 97–107
    returning, 107–11
    training of, 18, 54, 65, 72, 100–101
Volunteers in Service to America (VISTA), 63

War on Poverty, 53
Watergate scandal, 64
Water projects, 80, 85–86, 87, 92, 93
Wiggins, Warren, 39, 40, 41
Williams, Frank, 102
Williams, Robert R., 24, 25
Wofford, Harris, 39, 41, 72
World Bank, 93, 113
World Food Organization, 114
World Health Organization, 113
World War II, 23, 27, 37

Zaire, 85, 93

Madeline Weitsman, a free-lance writer in New York City, received a B.A. in psychology from Queens College and an M.A. in political science from the New School for Social Research. She was a reporter for the *Stamford Advocate* and the *New York Daily News*. She also worked as a legislative aide to two New York state senators and taught in the New York public school system for four years.

Arthur M. Schlesinger, jr., served in the White House as special assistant to Presidents Kennedy and Johnson. He is the author of numerous acclaimed works in American history and has twice been awarded the Pulitzer Prize. He taught history at Harvard College for many years and is currently Albert Schweitzer Professor of the Humanities at the City College of New York.